KU-478-526

GRAPHIC DESIGN
IN THE COMPUTER AGE
General Editor: André Jute

PRESENTATIONS
for professional communicators
Bill Murphy

Batsford

Contents

LEEDS BECKETT UNIVERSITY
LIBRARY
DISCARDED

Leeds Metropolitan University

17 0185514 7

Contents

4

Without whose assistance...

All illustrations are by Bill Murphy
exclusively in Adobe and Aldus
software, except crayon drawings
p13, pp 52-53, p55, p65
© Áine Watkins

Cover design and title page
by André Jute

Typeset and originated by
Create Colour Bureau, Bath
Printed in Singapore for the
publisher, B. T. Batsford Ltd
4 Fitzhardinge Street,
London W1H OAH

Text and illustrations
copyright © 1995
Bill Murphy
The right of
Bill Murphy to be
identified as the
author and illustrator
of this work has been
asserted in
accordance with the
Copyright, Designs
and Patents
Act 1988
ISBN 0 7134 7172 7
A CIP catalogue
record for this book
is available from the
British Library

All rights reserved. No
part of this book may be
reproduced or utilised in
any form or by any
means, electronic or
mechanical, including
photocopying, recording,
or by any information
storage and retrieval
systems, without
permission in writing
from the publisher.

LEEDS METROPOLITAN
UNIVERSITY LIBRARY
1701855147
E2-BV
651457 2·10·97
10·11·97
658.452 MUR

The Ogham Stone – Understood by all

The ancient Celtic race devised a written language which was called Ogham (pronounced 'ohm')

At the time the only medium of recording was on stone and this was certainly taken into consideration by the person who devised it.

Its beauty lay in its simplicity. There were just 20 letters (15 consonants and five vowels).It was understood by the vast majority of the Celtic population. No other written language in the world could make such a boast. Tribal chieftains could use it as boundary markers and be sure that all – friend and foe – would understand it.

Simplicity is the cornerstone on which I base all my presentations. No-one has ever complained to me that they were disappointed because they understood every word.

I don't have two vocabularies. Most people have a speaking vocabulary *and* a writing vocabulary. They use words in reports and letters that they would never dream of using in conversation.

Why?

Write as you would speak – and follow the simple, straightforward rules set out in this book and the presentation of your graphic designs will attain your objective.

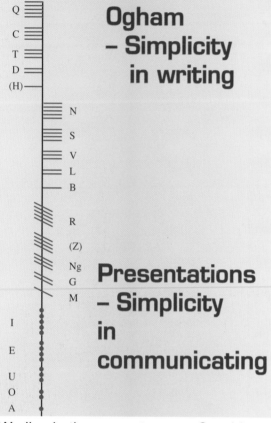

Ogham
– Simplicity
in writing

Presentations
– Simplicity
in
communicating

We live in the computer age. Graphic designers' imaginative concepts continuously push their hardware and software to the outer limits.

Nevertheless the product of their creative genius must be communicated to others. Many times this necessitates delivering their presentation to those of a more formal logical way of thinking.

Presentations must be structured. They must work within constraints of time and space and, indeed, understanding. They must ensure that their message is understood by all present. They must be simple, in the best sense of the word.

Delivering a successful presentation requires many skills.

Oratory: You must be able to speak with confidence in public.

Salesmanship: You must be able to convince your audience to take a certain course of action.

Showmanship: You must make it an enjoyable experience for your audience.

Delivery: It's not just what you say but how you say it.

Timing: You must say it within the allotted span.

Empathy: You must be at one with your audience. Always speak in a style that they will easily understand.

Despite all this, when would-be presenters think of a presentation they usually think in terms of the the actual visual aids. Professional lecturers are inclined to view it from a totally different aspect. They see the presentation in relation to themselves and their knowledge of the subject. Of course they can handle the task, don't they know ten times more about the subject than any one else who will be present? This is probably true.

The vast majority of lecturers know their subject intimately. They are usually chosen because they are experts or in their particular field. However they differ in at least one respect from teachers.

Teachers, as part of their training, are taught the art of communicating information to others. They realise that although they are experts in their particular subjects, their pupils may be hearing this particular lesson for the first time. Therefore they structure their lessons accordingly.

Lecturers are often completely unaware of the need to pace themselves according to the depth of knowledge of their audience. Very often they assume knowledge and familiarity with the subject far beyond the limits of their audience. This leads to confusion and other difficulties for the listener.

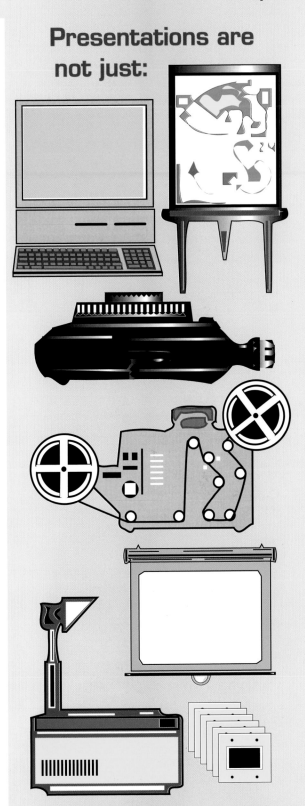

Presentations are not just:

If the visual aids are right, they imagine, then everything else will fall into place. The audience will be blinded to all other deficiencies.

You can have the most wonderful visual aids ever created and still your presentation can be nothing more than a complete flop!

But if, in your preparation, you take the audience level of understanding into positive consideration you are already on the road to success.

Once you do this all your preparation will be geared to the proper level of communication and your presentation will be understood.

This book looks at presentations from this angle. Just as, in writing, it is the reader who is the most important part of the equation, so it is in presentations. It is the listener who is vital. It is a sobering thought that without the audience, there would be no reason for you to be there in the first place.

We live in an age of total communication. We can have a simultaneous conversation with others in each of the five continents. There are heart transplants taking place in, say, Bombay, being overseen by specialists in South Africa and America.

And yet, at the same time, we live in an age where, at all levels, not enough consideration is given to ensuring that the message is being received properly.

One factory has this accident recorded:

An electrician put a sign 'hot' on a bare and protruding piece of metal.

A workman was 'careful' to equip himself with metal tongs before trying to pick it up. He, literally, got the shock of his life!

What had gone wrong? The electrician had assumed knowledge on behalf of those who would read the notice.

In his jargon, 'hot' meant 'live'. He assumed everyone would know this.

He should have asked himself:

Who will read this notice?
Will they understand what is meant? Remember, to an electrical engineer 'hot' means alive with electricity. To a metallurgist it may mean simply high in temperature. To some physicists, 'radioactive'. To some men the first thing to come to mind would be 'sexy'!

As a presenter you must never be guilty of assuming knowledge on the part of your audience.

Adopt the approach outlined in the following pages and you will increase your understanding of all the facets that go to make up a successful presentation.

Graphic designers are very creative people and the strictures attached to the actual preparation are off-putting. They see nothing but problems ahead. But classify these problems, understand the principles behind them and the task is not so daunting. there is even the opportunity to use their creativity.

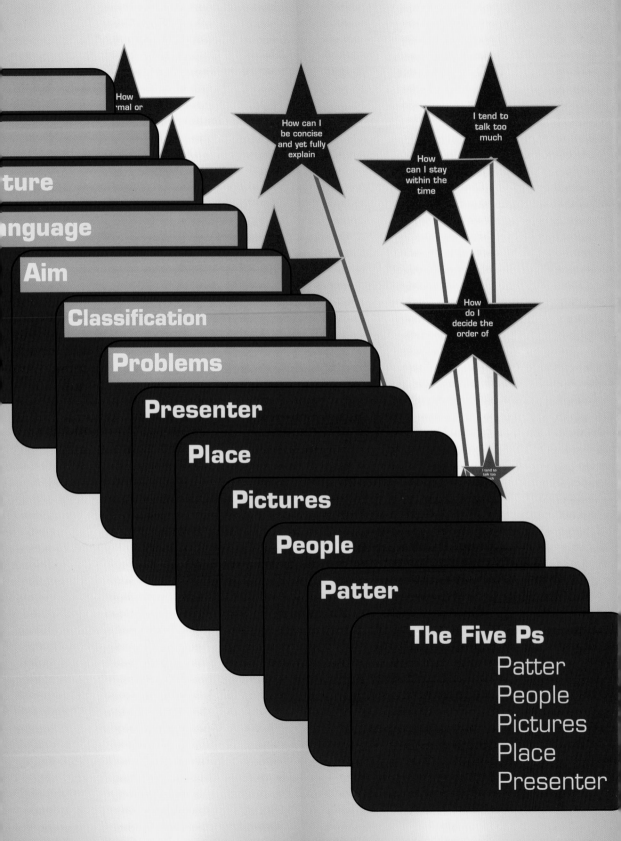

Problems...
Problems...
Problems

Think about it – your job as a presenter is, in the majority of cases, to solve the problems of your audience.

If it is a sales presentation, you are trying to show how your design will solve your client's problems.

If you are reporting to your Board of Directors, again, you will want to show how taking a certain course of action will solve some of the company's problems.

...And so on.

The best way to find out what the problems are is to ask the group directly. When running communications workshops for small groups I ask applicants to let me know what their major problems in this particular area are. They do this on the application form. I then summarize their replies and include them with the participants' notes.

With larger groups this is not possible but I do ask them to write out their three main problems on individual cards at the very start. These cards are gathered up and placed in a box. I point out that problems can be classified and once we understand the principles behind each classification, the solution is at hand. Then I choose cards at random from the box and we decide their classification. As we proceed through the principles we refer back to the individual problems on their cards and see if we now know the solution to the problem.

There are five facets to presentations – each one equally important.

They are listed alphabetically. No one takes precedence over another. Each is vital to the success of the whole.

The Five Ps

Patter
People
Pictures
Place
Presenter

Patter

Not only what you say, but how you say it is vital to your success

Patter

You must speak in a language that your audience will understand. Avoid jargon and, except with specialized groups, professional terms.

People

You must know your audience and speak to their interests. If the object of the exercise is to have your audience take a certain course of action, then you must speak in terms of interest to them.

People

You must know your audience and speak to its interests

Pictures

Your visual aids must sit comfortably both with your topic and your audience

Pictures

Here the colours used are also important. There are good colours to use as backgrounds. There are also good colours to use as emphasizers.

Place

If possible, get familiar with the auditorium beforehand

Place

If this is possible, you should make a point of visiting it and getting a 'feel' for the place.

You will know, roughly, the size of your audience. This will also influence the type of visual aids used.

Presenter

There is a lot of sense in the axiom that you are only as good as your last presentation. Remember this. The audience in front of you is the most important audience you have ever addressed. Never forget this.

Presenter

Reputations are made – and lost – from your performance 'on the night'

This book will deal with each one in turn as it looks at presentations under the five headings mentioned overleaf.

Its object is to make your presentation one that will be remembered and reacted to in the manner you intend.

Look at your own problems. Anything that irritates when preparing or communicating your presentation.

These problems may be classified neatly under one of five headings.

Problems

may be classified under five headings

Problem Classification

Aim
Language
Structure
Layout
Techniques

Some contain aspects of two of these headings. Rarely does a problem contain more than two of these elements.

There are problems in defining to whom the presentation should be aimed; how it should be targeted.

Aim

Problems in defining the purpose of the presentation

Language

Problems with deciding how to phrase your presentation

Some have problems deciding on the type of language to use. The object should be to express an idea or point of view clearly and simply, not to impress your listeners with your vocabulary.
You will never hear anyone complain because they have understood every word.

Structure: the disciplines attached to actually sitting down and writing out (or dictating) the presentation causes havoc to the free-spirit creative mind of the graphic artist. Crystallize these problems and you are more than half-way to their solution.

Structure

Problems associated with actually putting your delivery together

Layout

Problems in logically arranging all or aspects of your presentation

There are problems in deciding the actual layout: what should be stressed and where? How many different ways are there to layout a lecture or seminar?

Readers will be relieved to discover that there are but two.

Techniques encompass all other areas that go to ensure that your presentation will be the success you deserve.
Ways of ensuring you know when your audience is bored; using colour in your slides or overhead transparencies; loosening up a 'stiff' group or controlling one that seems to have become too obstreperous.

Techniques

Problems associated with delivery and audience reaction

All the little things that can cause problems if you are either unaware of them or do not know how to handle them. The problems that arise in making presentations can be classified under these headings.

The purpose of this book is to help presenters with their problems. It should be looked on as a tool to fine tune aspects with which you are not completely happy.

When conducting seminars or workshops I make a point of finding out the three main problems of the individuals attending. This information is easily gathered by putting the question on the application form. I summarize these anonymously and include them with the notes. No corrections or alterations are made. If there are some I don't understand, I ask the group, never the individual. That makes its own point.

Problems...
Problems...
Problems...

Then I ask the group to run down through the list and place an initial in the box identifying the type of problem it is. (ie **A**im, **L**anguage, **S**tructure, **L**ayout or **T**echnique). Over the period of the course most if not all these problems will be solved by dealing with the principles involved.

Here are some actual problems identified at a recent workshop entitled "Who trains the trainer?" Notice how the same problem can originate from different sources.

Being concise and to the point	
Choice of words in preferring one sentence, phrase instead of another	
Stating clearly and precisely the effect which a particular action has	
Order in which points should be made	
Deciding on what points should be included	
Concise format	
Meaningful expression	
Adequate summary	
My main problem is deciding to what extent one is to expand in technical terms	
It is difficult to be concise as regards content and lucid as regards style	
Concluding on areas without bringing in irrelevancies	

Conciseness. I tend to get involved in unnecessarily lengthy explanations ☐

When to adopt a formal style and when an easier style ☐

Deciding on the amount of information to include and the order ☐

Not being able to accurately describe and a tendency to ramble ☐

Summarizing the important points ☐

I have a tendency to talk too much ☐

Taking two or three sentences to say what could probably be said in one ☐

I have a difficulty in expressing concepts clearly ☐

I understand the concept but have great difficulty in getting it across to others ☐

When to adopt a formal style and when to use an easier style ☐

Difficulty in making concise points without rambling ☐

It is difficult to know when to use a formal style or a simple style ☐

In order to explain fully and in understandable language I often talk too much ☐

I tend to get involved in unnecessarily lengthy explanations with participants ☐

Deciding how much time I should devote to a particular aspect. ☐

The amount of information to include and the order in which it is to be included ☐

I find it hard to know when to adopt a format style or an easier style ☐

Write down three of the problems you personally experience and see under which of the headings they fall. In this way you will subconsciously personalize your reading and set your own objectives.

At the end you will be able to attack the difficulties you experience in a positive manner.

Let's lay it all out graphically overleaf…

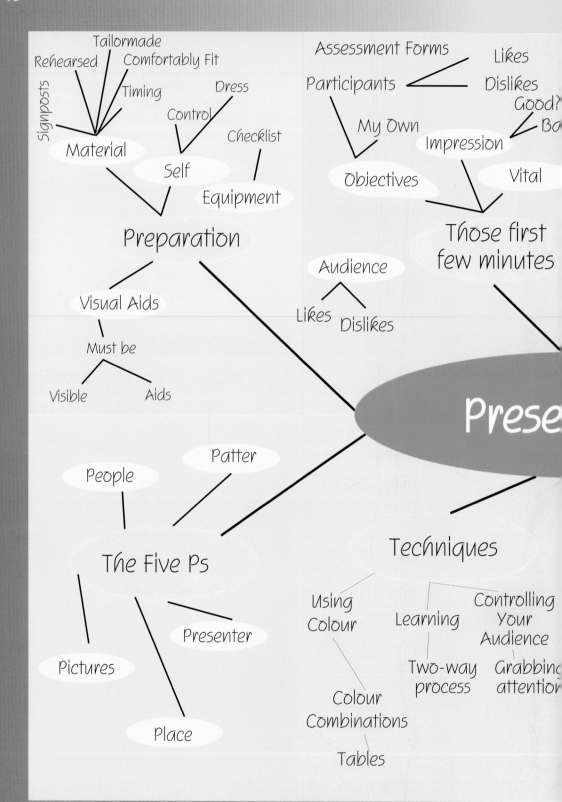

Questions — How? — Kipling

To tell — To sell — Clarify

My own

For Group

Aim

Paragraphs — Verbal Noun — Passive

Sentences — Long — Verb

Words

Difficult

Avoid jargon

Language — Cliches

Keep it Simple

Avoid Like the Plague!!

cations

Structure

Aim?

Layout

Sell? — Tell?

Check Aim

The Rule of Six

Audience Size

...ype

Visual Aids

...Must be Visible — Must be Aids!

The 6 Steps

Sell — Tell

Why — What

What — Why

Aim?
Jot Down
Group
Discard
Write Out
Reread & Polish

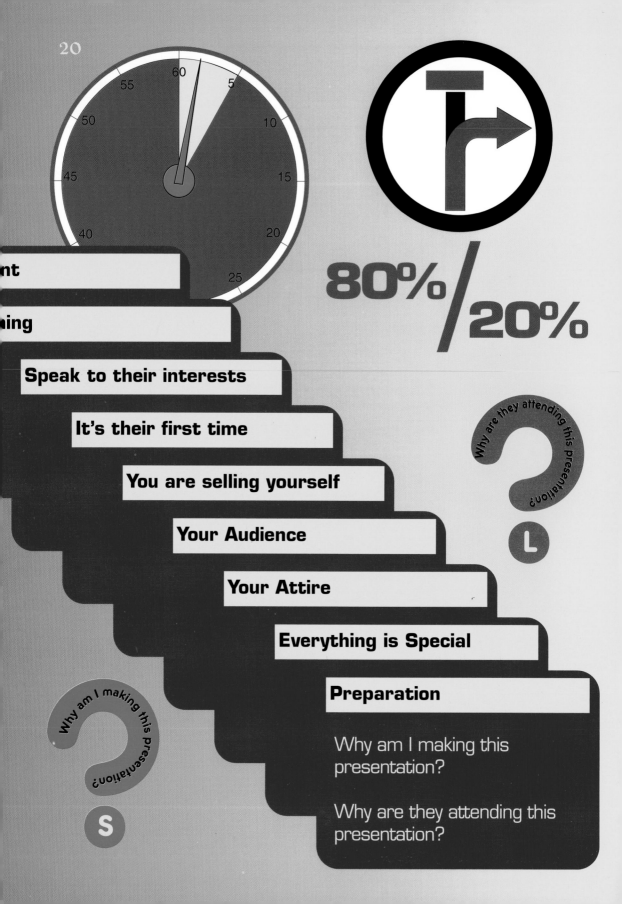

Preparation

The 'It-will-be-all-right-on-the-night'-attitude to presentations has ruined many reputations. Indeed, it has turned many who might have been excellent in the role away from a career that can give great personal satisfaction.

Because of a nail a shoe was lost…
…Because of a messenger a kingdom was lost…
…And all because a nail was lost

Success in presentation begins with the preparation; with taking pains to cover every aspect in detail; with the objective of sending your audience away truly satisfied that they have benefited from the experience – and look forward to returning to hear you again. Approach your preparation in this frame of mind and, where your audience is concerned, never be satisfied with giving them second best.

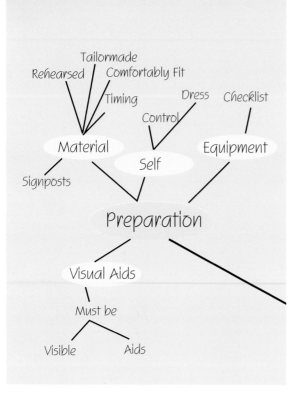

Your personal objective will not be achieved unless your group has absolute confidence in you as a speaker.

Ninety per cent of your audience will spend at least the first half an hour (if not the total time up to the first official "break") doing nothing else but sizing you up.

They will not be prepared to give you their full attention until they have decided that you are competent to deliver the presentation which they are attending.

This is why
- your appearance
- your punctuality in commencing
- your opening greeting
- everything done during the first part of the first session is vital to the success of the total presentation.

You are and must remain the focus of attention throughout.

Nothing must detract or distract from this.

Preparation is the key. Sound preparation gives you inner confidence.

This reflects on your audience and gives them confidence in you.

You are and must remain the focus of attention throughout

PREPARATION

The secret of every successful project – preparation.

Ask yourself the question, "Why am I making this presentation?"

Then, "Why is my audience attending?"

Preparation

Why am I making this presentation?
Why are they attending this presentation?

The answers to both these questions are crucial to your success.

You must write them down. Doing this crystallizes the answers.

If your presentation is one that is applied for, have the question on the application form – Why are you attending this presentation?

In this way you will know, even as you prepare, the aspirations of those attending.

Preparation

Knowing why they are attending means you are forearmed.

Where applicable, hand out the assessment at the beginning. Point out that one of the questions the participants must answer before they leave is, "Have you achieved your own objectives for the course?"

Many of those attending are there because they have been 'sent'. Answering such questions for themselves at the beginning gives them a far more positive attitude to the presentation. This can only assist you.

YOUR CLOTHES:

Never arrive for a presentation without having had a bath that day. Everything you wear should be freshly laundered or cleaned and pressed. Your shoes will be gleaming and pockets emptied of all but the bare necessities.

Why?

Because then you know that there is absolutely nothing amiss with the person you are presenting to your audience.

You are as presentable as can be and so can concentrate on the substance of the presentation without any distractions.

Your Attire

☑ – Everything must be fresh
☑ – Shoes gleaming
☑ – Pockets emptied
Then...
You don't have to worry about your appearance – you can concentrate on the presentation

Everything is Special

☑ The presentation is special
☑ The visual aids are special
☑ The manual is special
☑ – And *you are* special

Your audience must know that *everything* about this presentation is special.

If they have this impression, they will be far more inclined to learn and benefit from the presentation.

– And, after all, that is the important thing – that they go away both enlightened and confident to handle an area of their work that caused some problems for them in the past.

YOUR AUDIENCE

Remember that, although you may have made this presentation many times, it will be the first time that this particular group has heard it

The dialogue must always be aimed towards this particular audience.

Your Audience

- ☑ – Type
- ☑ – What are their interests
- ☑ – What action/reaction do you require

Vary your dialogue to take into consideration the composition of your audience.

Your objective will be the same for most audiences but the dialogue and visual aids may differ.

Your Audience

- ☑ – Remember all the time that you are selling yourself.
- ☑ – that you will be judged by many on your last presentation

Your Audience

It may be the hundredth time you have given this presentation but it will be the first time your audience has heard it

It is vital to determine

1 – The type of people
2 – Their interests
3 – What action or reaction you want

The answer to 3 may be the same in each case, but 1 and 2 must vary the content of your delivery.

Your Audience

- ☑ – Speak to their interests
- ☑ – Speak in a manner that will be easily understood by them
- ☑ – Involve your audience by 'speaking in questions'

You are only as good as your last presentation.

Gear the content to the audience. If this entails changing the dialogue, do so. If this means remaking some (or all) visual aids, then do so.

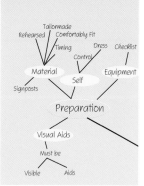

YOUR MATERIAL

Your material must be tailor-made for that particular audience.

When the dialogue and the visual aids are prepared they must be rehearsed together and timed to ensure that each session *will comfortably fit* within the allotted time span.

Be prepared for 'diversions'. They may be caused by a member being unable to understand a particular concept. They may be caused by you being 'side-tracked'.

Whatever the reason, you must catch up on your own timetable without encroaching on the group's free time.

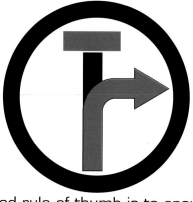

A good rule of thumb is to ensure what you have to deliver actually takes up only 80% of the allotted session time.

Now you can cover additional questions and explanations without feeling that such questions are eating into the time you need to successfully conclude your session.

Have your timetable show where you ought to be at any specific time.

If you keep referring to this regularly you can make any adjustments necessary as the session proceeds – and you know the time position on a continuous basis.

Timing

- ☑ Allow for interruptions
- ☑ Fill only 80% of the allotted time
- ☑ Never infringe on candidates' free time

VISUAL AIDS

Some presenters have favourite slides that they are particularly proud of. Sometimes they will impose these on a program although the relevance is often doubtful. Never be guilty of this.

Visual Aids

- ☑ – Must be visible
- ☑ – Must be aids – to this particular topic

Visual Aids

- ☑ – Never fill the whole area of the slide
- ☑ – Remember these slides are aids – they are never intended to take your place

The crime is often compounded by the lecturer actually remarking, "I don't suppose you can read this but…"

If he doesn't suppose you can understand it, it shouldn't have been used in the first place.

Part of my time is spent evaluating lecturers.

Many times I see professionals placing an overhead transparency of a full page of writing onto the overhead projector and expecting the audience to be able to read it.

Visual Aids

Check out your own visual aids:

- ☑ – Are they relevant to this particular audience?
- ☑ – Are they suitable for this particular auditorium?

Visual Aids

If you can't readily understand them – and you designed or made them – what chance has someone seeing them for the first time?

Run through your own visual aids some time before the date of the presentation – if possible in the actual room or theatre you will use. See whether, by sitting in various different seats in the auditorium, you can read and understand your own visual aids.

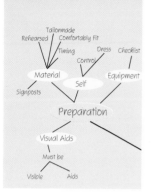

YOUR EQUIPMENT

Many times I bless the man who thought up Murphy's Law because knowing it makes me that little bit more careful.

I physically check all my equipment one week before the date of the presentation. I check it again on the day before – and check it one more time if it has to be transported to a different location.

Because of a nail a shoe was lost...
...Because of a messenger a kingdom was lost...
...And all because a nail was lost

Part of my standard equipment is spares. Here is my checklist:

Ball-point pens.	❑
Blue-tack	❑
Business cards	❑
Chalk – coloured + white	❑
Drawing pins	❑
Electrical multi-plugs (or adaptor-plugs)	❑
Extension cables	❑
Flipchart pads	❑
Manuals	❑
Notebooks	❑
Pencils	❑
Polo Mints	❑
Small change (coins) for telephones	❑
Spare blank transparencies	❑
Spare bulb for overhead projector	❑
Spare fuses for plugs	❑
Spare pens for dry-wipe boards and flip charts	❑
Spare pens (permanent)	❑
Spare pens (washable)	❑
Tissues (Someone always has a cold!)	❑

The list may seem overcautious but, remember that the majority of the items must be gathered only once and are then available for all time.

Rarely do I have to resort to my spares bag but, on the odd occasion when it is necessary, it has meant the difference between a successful presentation and a fiasco.

If equipment is being supplied make sure all is in prefect working order.

The Venue

Check:
- ✓ – Position of power points
- ✓ – Are leads long enough
- ✓ – Check local fire regulations and positions of all exits
- ✓ – Is furniture arranged?

It is this attention to detail that ensures the success of your presentation. Many will judge you on this presentation alone – and you don't get a second chance to make a first impression.

All your problems can be solved if you examine them individually in a clinical fashion.

Write down the answers to the following questions and you will find that you are more than half way towards a solution.

Equipment

- ✓ – Have a checklist
- ✓ – If equipment is hired, make sure it is tested well before performance time.

Inspect the room or theatre where the presentation will be delivered.

Note the position of all power points and the distances between them and where you intend siting your equipment. Make sure your equipment leads are long enough.

The Presentation

If everything goes according to plan, no-one will probably notice the pains you have taken to ensure this.
But...

What is the problem?

What are the causes of this problem?

What are possible solutions to this problem?

What, in your opinion, is the best solution to this problem?

Participants Dislike

- Being ignored
- Feeling 'lost'
- Shoddiness

Participants also dislike

- Unpunctuality
- lack of professionalism on the part of the presenter

Participants Like

- A professional air
- To feel presenter is in control
- To know times of breaks

Participants Like

(Small Groups)
- To be greeted
- Presenter to use their names
- To know who is sitting beside them

Those First Few Minutes

"That is most unfair!"is the usual reaction from any group when it is pointed out that the majority of participants form a very decided opinion about their presenter during the first four minutes.

Unfortunately it is true, and fairness does not come into it.

We all react to a stranger or a newcomer and it takes quite a while to change that reaction. This is why it is vital to be conscious of audience likes and dislikes. This is why a separate section has been devoted to this aspect of presentations.

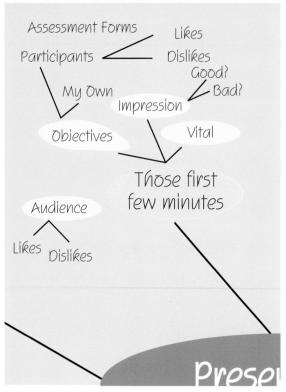

Assessment Forms — Likes

Participants — Dislikes

Good?
Bad?

My Own
Impression

Objectives

Vital

Those first
few minutes

Audience

Likes Dislikes

Prese

THE FIRST FEW MINUTES

The first few minutes of the first session are the most vital of all. Your audience began forming an opinion of you as soon as they saw you or as soon as you were identified to them as 'the speaker'.

Will this opinion be favourable or unfavourable?

Will you be starting the session with your audience behind you? Or will you be attempting to claw your way back to square one without even knowing it?

Knowing their likes and dislikes can be very helpful in this situation.

Nothing can be considered as trivial if its effect can contribute towards the bonding of (or driving a wedge between) presenter and listener. Unless your audience feels 'comfortable' with you, it will not be inclined to give you the trust you require to get difficult concepts across.

Participants Like

- A professional air
- To feel presenter is in control
- To know times of breaks
- To know the 'ground rules'

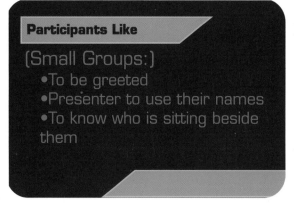

Participants Like

(Small Groups:)
- To be greeted
- Presenter to use their names
- To know who is sitting beside them

All participants like to know the times and durations of breaks. They secretly object when these times are encroached upon. Small groups like the presenter to use their names. They also like to know the names of others when discussing various points. A simple and legible name card can take care of this.

Anything that upsets the candidates in the least way will reflect on you. Therefore the buck stops with you.

You must be at the venue well before time.

You must ensure that the room or theatre is prepared and open on time.

> Our Guest speaker for this evening needs no introduction
> - He didn't show up!

Let them know from the outset that they are dealing with a professional who respects those who attended so punctually.

You must check that there are sufficient course materials for all attending.

Greet each one cheerily. If a bottle-neck should occur make sure you know how to assist the registrar to relieve the situation.

The majority of those attending will arrive during the last few minutes, so make the necessary arrangements to cope with this.

Five minutes before commencement time you will be inside the lecture theatre to ensure that no last-minute hitches have occurred there. On the stroke of commencement time, begin.

Participants Dislike

- Being ignored
- Feeling 'lost'
- Shoddiness
- Incompetence
- Being made to look or feel a fool

PARTICIPANTS DISLIKE:
Knowing the dislikes of participants is as important as knowing what they like.

Remember that, particularly during the first session, it is very easy to upset them. Give them a little time to settle in.

Participants also dislike

- Unpunctuality
- Lack of professionalism on the part of the presenter
- Presenters who 'over-run'

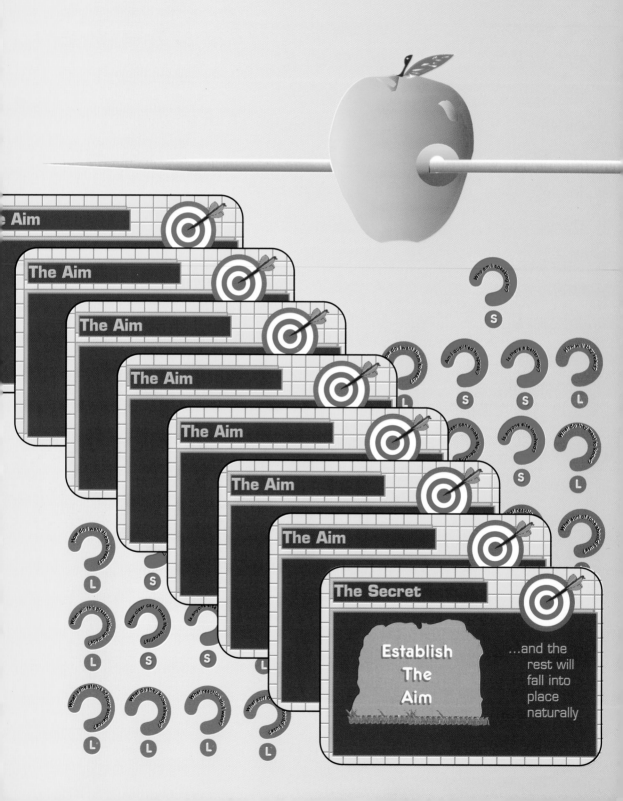

The Aim

If someone has trouble with structuring or laying out a presentation, the chances are that they will be aware of this.

A person may have difficulty in the aim area and not be even conscious that it is where the problem is.

Aim is all about defining your objectives and deciding the best way of achieving them.

Among the items you must know are:
- What you want to achieve
- How you are going to achieve it
- Who your audience is

Establishing the aim is all about answering questions - the right questions...

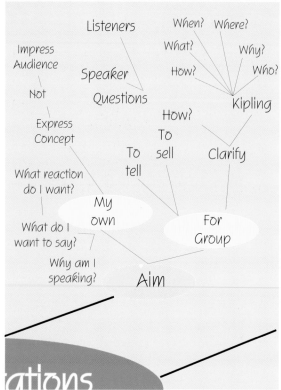

THE AIM

All presentations are either giving information or endeavouring to persuade a group to take a certain course of action.

Either you want to tell them something or sell them something.

The majority would, I imagine, come under the second heading.

Examples of information presentations can range from the showing of your holiday slides to friends to an attempt to explain Einstein's Theory of Relativity.

The persuasion presentation can range from an appeal to a group to take a certain course of action to an educational seminar.

There is a very interesting book entitled "If you don't know where you're going, you may end up someplace else!" The same could very well be said about writing in general and presentations in particular.

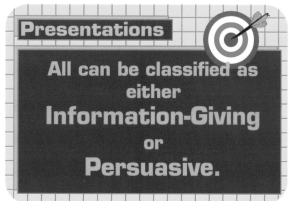

UNLESS YOU HAVE DECIDED:

– **Exactly why you are giving this presentation, what you want to say and what reaction you want –**
you stand an excellent chance of *not* achieving your objective.
Establish clearly and precisely at the outset exactly why you are making this presentation.
As you will see, if this is done, the other principles will fall more readily into place.

THE FIRST RULE OF PRESENTATIONS IS TO ESTABLISH THE AIM.

This will make sure that you communicate most effectively and efficiently with the listeners.

HOW TO CLARIFY THE AIM

Here are some questions to ask yourself:

Am I qualified to speak on this subject? .... ✓
Why speak at all? .... ✓
Do I have to? .... ✓
Is there a better way? .... ✓
Who am I speaking to? .... ✓
What is their status? .... ✓
Is anyone else involved? .... ✓
What do they want to know? .... ✓
What do they know already? .... ✓
How will they react? .... ✓
How do I want them to react? .... ✓
What sort of tone should I use? .... ✓
How clear can I make the benefits? .... ✓
When will this presentation be made? .... ✓
Where will the presentation be made? .... ✓
– Home or Abroad? .... ✓

There are more Aim Questions affecting the listener than the speaker. This should also bring home to you that the important factor in the presentation is the audience. After all, without the audience, there would be no need for you to be there at all.

Your objective is **not to impress but to express** an idea, or a point of view, or persuade the group to take a certain course of action.

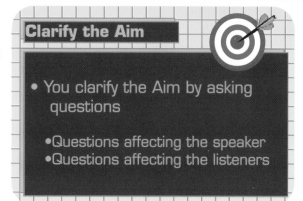

Clarify the Aim

- You clarify the Aim by asking questions

  •Questions affecting the speaker
  •Questions affecting the listeners

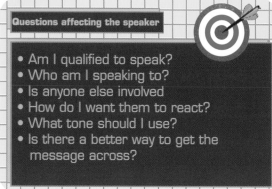

Questions affecting the speaker

- Am I qualified to speak?
- Who am I speaking to?
- Is anyone else involved
- How do I want them to react?
- What tone should I use?
- Is there a better way to get the message across?

This must be accomplished in a manner and a language that your audience will understand comfortably.

The answers to the 'Aim Questions' will influence the language, structure, layout and techniques used.

Make sure you do cover all the questions that will give you indications of what your audience requires. If there is an application form and you require answers to specific questions, you can include these on the form.

Using pattern notes, have a brain storming session with yourself. The question you pose is important here.

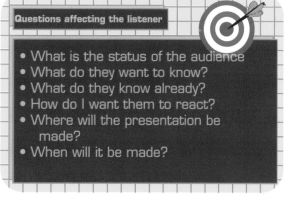

Questions affecting the listener

- What is the status of the audience
- What do they want to know?
- What do they know already?
- How do I want them to react?
- Where will the presentation be made?
- When will it be made?

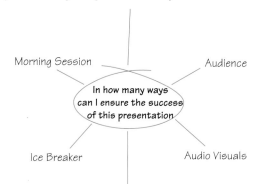

A question like "How can I make sure this presentation is a success?" implies that there is but one correct answer and stunts creativity. Prefixing the question with a phrase like "In how many ways..." tells you immediately that there is far more than one right answer.

The Secret

Establish
The
Aim

...and the rest will fall into place naturally

The secret to successful presentations lies more with establishing the aim than any other single factor.

– And the only way of establishing the aim is to ask questions. Never assume. It is very often just an easy excuse not to take pains.

Rudyard Kipling put it succinctly.

"Without questions my dispatches would never have reached the dispatch bag."

He even wrote a little poem about it:

Six Serving Men

I keep six honest serving men
(They taught me all I knew)
Their names
> Are What?
> And Why?
> And When?
> And How?
> And Where?
> And Who?

"I keep six honest serving men
They taught me all I knew.
Their names are What and Why
And When and How and Where and Who."

Use these six serving men and you must hit the bull's eye every time.

Unless you have decided:

- **Exactly why you are giving this presentation?**

- **What you want to say?**

- **What reaction you want from the audience?**

You stand an excellent chance of *not* achieving your objective

Remember that the answer lies in questions...

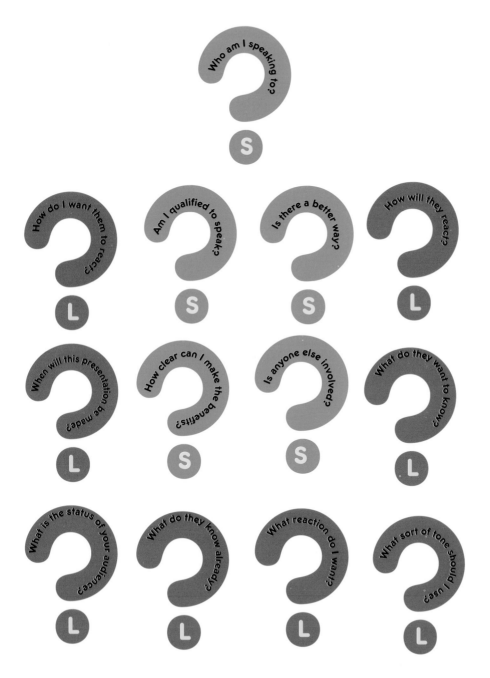

...and there are far more questions affecting the listener.

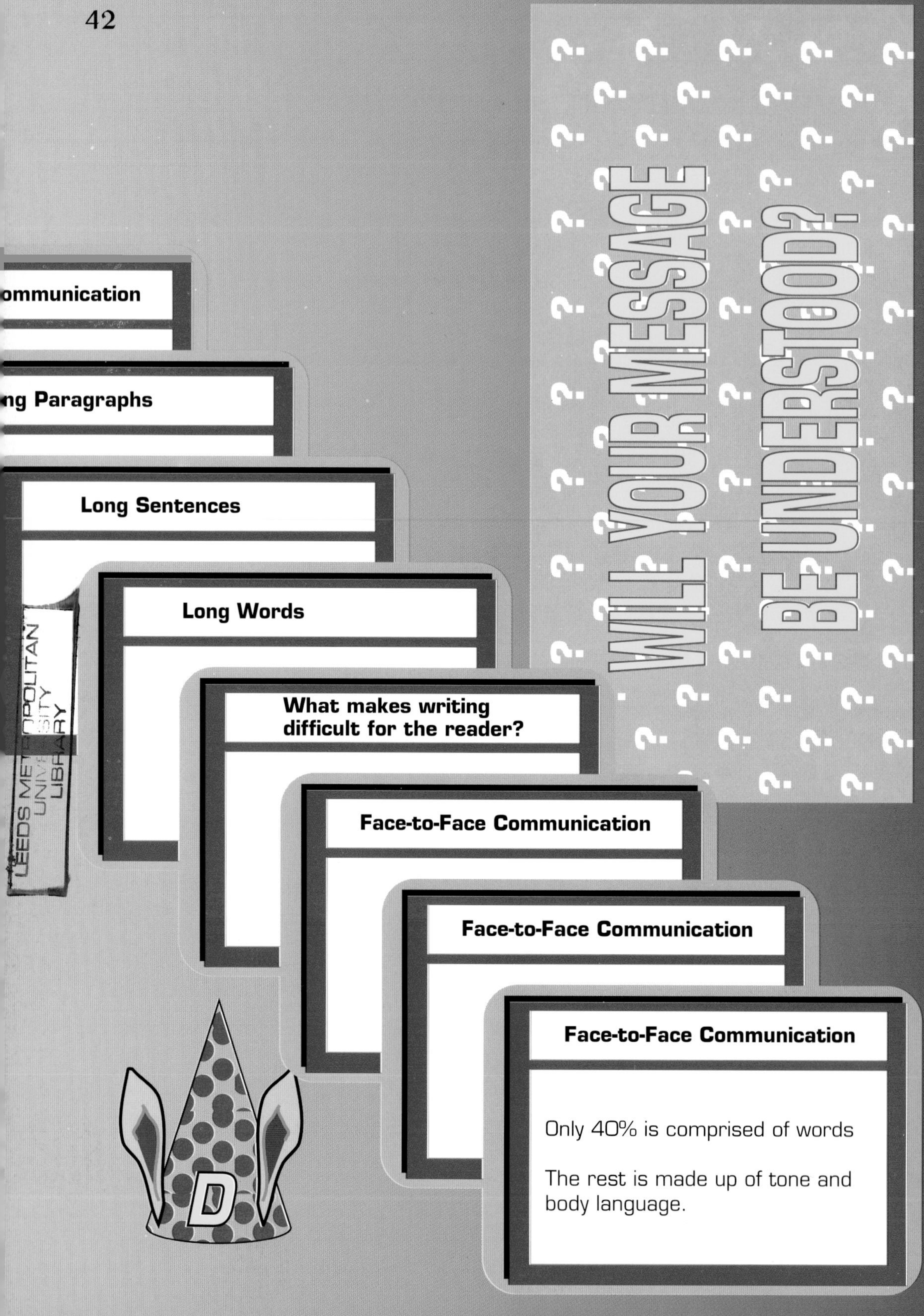

WILL YOUR MESSAGE BE UNDERSTOOD?

ommunication

ng Paragraphs

Long Sentences

Long Words

LEEDS METROPOLITAN UNIVERSITY LIBRARY

What makes writing difficult for the reader?

Face-to-Face Communication

Face-to-Face Communication

Face-to-Face Communication

Only 40% is comprised of words

The rest is made up of tone and body language.

D

Language

The presentation, to be successful, must be delivered in the language of the audience. The delivery must be easily understood and not clouded by jargon or terms unfamiliar to the listeners.. The tense of verb employed will also contribute towards the ease or difficulty of the script.

If we are conscious of what makes speaking or reading difficult to understand and assimilate, we are well on our way towards presenting a session that will be both easily understood and enjoyable.

With the Clarity Index it is possible actually to measure the degree of difficulty of the script.

Rehearsal is vital, not only for timing but also to determine that what you have prepared can be delivered with ease.

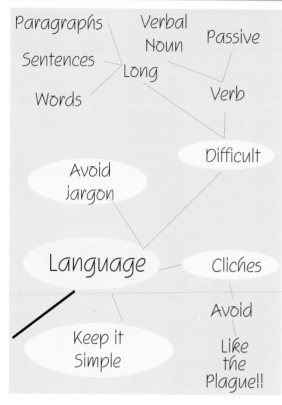

It's often said that Britain and America are two countries divided by a common language.

The same could be said of the relationship between presenter and audience. This is particularly so in what might be described as technical presentations. The presenter forgets his audience is not as familiar with technical terms as those in the circles he or she normally frequents.

A designer reporting to a client may be oblivious of the fact that the majority of the audience comes from non-design backgrounds. Everyday design terms (to him) may be as greek to them.

The fear of seeming a fool will prevent many from pointing out they they do not understand what is being discussed.

Throw your mind back to your own schooldays. Remember the teacher, having explained some complex part of a lesson, would end by saying something like, "Do you all understand what I've done?"

–And you would find yourself nodding your head although, had he been speaking in Swahili, you could not have understood less. Yet the fear of being the only hand to go up and therefore seeming a fool prevented you from saying this.

This is why establishing the aim is so crucial to all the other facets that make up a successful presentation.

When you speak, it is not only the words you use that are important but how you deliver them.

Less than 40% of face to face communication is composed of the words you use. The rest (the majority) is comprised of tone and body language.

Face-to-Face Communication

Only 40% is comprised of words.

The rest is made up of tone and body language.

Face-to-Face Communication

From the moment you appear in front of your audience, they begin to react.
Before you say a word, you have created an impression.
– Is it good? – or bad?

Your presence, the confidence (or, indeed, lack of confidence) you evoke in your listeners (and watchers) – all will contribute to the overall impression you make.

In presentations you must deal, not only with the spoken word, but also with the written word.

Both media must be clearly understood. There must be clarity in your speech, in the visual aids, in the manuals or the notes that form part of the total package. Where manuals and course notes are concerned, it is vital that what is set down is written in a simple, easy-to-understand language.

Face-to-Face Communication

In presentations your audience has to deal with both the spoken word and the written word.

Understanding difficulties with writing helps all communication.

How can we be sure that what we prepare adheres to these principles?

Simply by understanding what makes writing difficult for the reader and applying these principles to all aspects of the preparation of the presentation.

One of your primary aims must be to express yourself, both in your writings and your delivery in simple, easy-to-understand English.

I don't think anyone has ever objected because they understood every word in a seminar or workshop.

Reading is recognizing words and knowing their meaning.
Listening is recognizing words and knowing their meaning.

What makes writing difficult for the reader?

☑ – Long Words
☑ – Long Sentences
☑ – Long Paragraphs
☑ – The verb case used
☑ – Jargon

WHAT WAS WRITTEN:

This report is to provide a comprehensive review of the work in order to point out the importance of quality control, as it pertains to the movement of the product through a factory, and to outline the different stages of growth through which the means of coping with the problem have progressed during the last ten years.

One sentence: total 56 words.

WHAT HE SAID:

This report has two aims:

Firstly, it shows the importance of quality control of a product as it moves through the factory.

Secondly, it outlines stages of growth of quality control during the last ten years.

Three sentences:
total 36 words.

WHAT WAS WRITTEN:

From the First Appalachian Conference on Behavioural Neuro-Dynamics: Walter Freeman has extended his earlier work on chaotic processing dynamics in the olfactory valve of rabbits.

His latest investigation concerns Intentionality in Hedgehogs. He concludes that they do use semantic concepts but their facial processing patterns are dependent on sensory input.

WHAT HE MEANT:

Hedgehogs stop moving if you block up their nostrils.

PEOPLE CHANGE

They normally talk simply and clearly. Ask them to express their views formally in front of an audience or write down their thoughts and things go wrong.

Many have two distinct vocabularies. Their normal conversational speech is quite ordinary and understandable. The vocabulary on which they draw for writing can be, to say the least archaic.

The table on the right is just to make you think. No one of these would make a big difference but a number of them can help to cloud what might otherwise be a simple message.

We say	We write
About	Approximately
After	Subsequent to
Best	Optimum
But, however	Nevertheless
Buy	Purchase
Carry out	Implement
End	Terminate
Keep up	Continue
Make easier	Facilitate
Need	Requirement
Show	Demonstrate
Since	In as much as
So…	Accordingly
So…	Consequently
Start, begin	Activate
Stop	Discontinue
Try	Endeavour
Use	Utilize

Long Words

- Don't deliberately use long words
- Use words with precise meanings
- Use a short word (or two or three) instead of a long word
- You may use up to 10% long words if you are sure they will be understood.

LONG WORDS

Words of three syllables or more can be more difficult to read and understand. Words not used often are not recognized as quickly. Readability suffers. This interferes with your ultimate objectives – perfect delivery and being easily understood by your audience.

LONG SENTENCES

Twenty copies of the memo on the right were sent out. The Personnel Manager received 18 phone calls asking what he meant!

We can wonder what exactly the other two District Managers did!

A Notice About Overtime

'When such conditions arise which requires work outside an employee's regular schedule and such work is estimated to require a full shift of eight hours or more on two or more consecutive scheduled days, even though unscheduled days intervene, an employee's hours of work will be charged as to include the hours when such work must be done, unless conditions do not permit the employee's absence from his previously scheduled hours.

Long sentences are usually caused by one of three reasons. The writer does not realize the trouble they cause. He is still thinking as he writes or using the wrong verb.

Long Sentences

Long sentences make understanding difficult
They are caused by:

- Being ignorant of their effect
- Still thinking while writing
- Using the wrong type of verb

Long Paragraphs

- Make writing look difficult

- Subconsciously put the reader off

LONG PARAGRAPHS

Readers react to writing before it is actually read. Long paragraphs make writing 'look' difficult to read. The reader is put off before the text is ever read. The paragraph should be a single theme with one principal and some subsidiary sentences.

As a general rule of thumb, limit your paragraphs to a maximum of six sentences.
Where paragraphs tend to be of more than this, examine them. Likely as not you will find that there is more than one theme within that paragraph.

Paragraphs

- A paragraph is a single theme with just one principal sentence and three or for subsidiary sentences

Long words confuse...

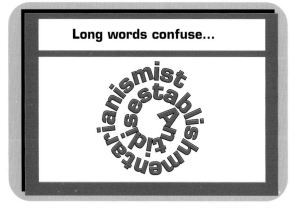

Everything said here about language applies equally to the spoken word. Long words can be difficult to pronounce and understand. Long sentences are difficult to deliver and understand. The listener is confused and there is a greater danger of you losing your 'train of thought'.

JARGON

Avoid jargon or technical and professional words which the listener or reader may not understand.

In 1949 Sir Ernest Gowers, in his invaluable guide to clear concise English, "The Complete Plain Words", gave us the Jargon Generator. It is a boon to those who would rather confuse than express themselves in clear English, which could be understood by all.

THE JARGON GENERATOR

The procedure is simple. All you do is think of a three-digital number at random and take the corresponding word from each column below. Thus 601 gives you the buzz-phrase, 'optimal management flexibility', 095 gives you 'integrated policy concept', 352 gives you 'parallel logistical capability', and so on.

	COLUMN 1		COLUMN 2		COLUMN 3
0	integrated	0	management	0	options
1	overall	1	organisational	1	flexibility
2	systematised	2	monitored	2	capability
3	parallel	3	reciprocal	3	mobility
4	functional	4	digital	4	programming
5	responsive	5	logistical	5	concept
6	optimal	6	transitional	6	time-phase
7	synchronised	7	incremental	7	projection
8	compatible	8	third generation	8	hardware
9	balanced	9	policy	9	contingency

So wrote Sir Ernest. His book was first written in 1949 and is still available. Gobbledygook has made great strides since then.

It is very easy to fall into the trap unless you are aware of it at all times.

Now you are armed to go forth and befuddle an already reeling world if you so wish.

Or, with a little forethought for your audience, write and speak simply and clearly – and always get your message across.

WHAT DO THEY MEAN?

It is not only jargon that causes trouble in communication.

You must be sure you know the exact meaning of the words you use. You must also feel confident that your audience knows their meaning. Otherwise you cannot be sure you are getting your message across.

Here are some words that you see often and probably use. Which of the alternatives 'a' to 'e' best fits each word? Ask your friends what they think. Will they all agree with you?

DEFINITIVE

a. certain
b. precise
c. conclusive
d. final
e. unchangeable

ENABLE

a. make possible
b. allow
c. make able
d. admit
e. excuse

INFER

a. make a statement
b. assume
c. imply a fact
d. decide
e. be led to believe

DIVERGENT

a. alternative
b. different
c. moving apart
d. divorced from
e. at odds with

OPTIMISE

a. hope for the best
b. maximise
c. use in the best way
d. make cheaply
e. compromise

FEASIBLE

a. probable
b. possible, but unlikely
c. plausible
d. practical
e. practicable

ECONOMIC

a. profitable
b. cheap
c. frugal
d. paying for itself
e. viable

REDUNDANT

a. inappropriate
b. unemployed
c. superfluous
d. dismissed
e. unnecessary

VIABLE

a. competitive
b. practicable
c. economic
d. economical
e. capable of independent growth

PROPOUND

a. suggest
b. add weight to
c. mix together
d. argue about
e. formulate

QUALITY OR QUANTITY?

In the Ten Commandments there are 299 words.
In a recent European Community directive on the grading of hen eggs there are more than 25,000 words!

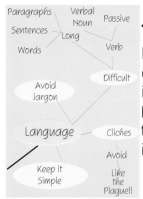

THE VERB

If there is one part of speech that influences clarity (or lack of it) more than any other, it is the verb.

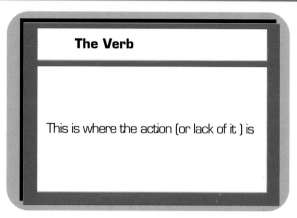

The Verb

This is where the action (or lack of it) is

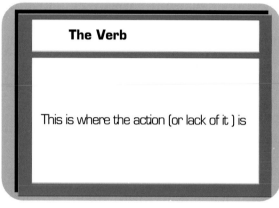

The Verb

This is where the action (or lack of it) is

Nothing can affect the length of a sentence more than the type of verb used. It is the most important part of the sentence. It generally conveys action.

Its misuse contributes more to failures in communication than any other part of speech.

There are three types of verb:

THE ACTIVE VERB

This is direct and concise.

Bill kissed Marilyn.

Just three words but the meaning is absolutely clear. There is no doubt or ambiguity about it .

THE PASSIVE VERB

Marilyn was kissed by Bill.

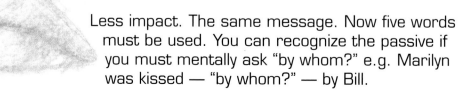

Less impact. The same message. Now five words must be used. You can recognize the passive if you must mentally ask "by whom?" e.g. Marilyn was kissed — "by whom?" — by Bill.

But often the writer forgets to answer it and this leads to confusion!

in the event of a strike, road transport will be supplied

—"by whom?"—no answer!

The reader or listener does not know who is going to take the action. He will have to spend time finding out.

THE VERBAL NOUN

This is dull and verbose. If your objective is to confuse, there is no better way than using quantities of verbal nouns.

The kissing of Marilyn was carried out by Bill.

Now the words have risen to nine but the message has suffered.

Keep the language simple. Remember your brief should be to express ideas clearly — not to try to impress people with your verbosity.

No-one has ever complained because the lecture or writing was so simple (in the very best sense) that they understood every word.

There is yet another impediment to clear writing and clear speech which has become even more prevalent during the nineties. This is the cliche.

Its cause may be that broadcast interviewers want their answers in a limited number of seconds. It may also be that people like politicians are more interested in fudging issues. Whatever the reason, the English language is being mangled out of recognition and the ensuing gobbledygook is helping to confuse even further.

Avoid phrases like:

… a game of two halves	… hearing what you have to say
… a level playing field	… in the fullness of time
… at this point in time	… moving goal posts
… bridge the gap	… the bottom line
… fatally flawed	… the jury is still out
… for good measure	… the way forward
… flavour of the month	… under active consideration
… get a result	… what you are really saying is
… have taken on board	… whole new ball game

"At this point in time, what's the difference between a duck?"

Phrases like these mean nothing but sound meaningful. They do nothing to add clarity or information to the subject being discussed. They do however, act as 'escape clauses' for those who like to comment and say nothing.

"The jury is still out on that one but I think one of its legs are both the same!"

In a recent BBC news program the phrase '… the way forward' was heard four times during different interviews – in political, technological, educational(!) and religious contexts.

Remember that you, as presenter, are there to 'express', not to impress your captive audience. It is your job to explain any aspect of the subject under discussion to your audience.

There will of course be times when you are asked a question to which you don't know the answer. When this occurs, face up to it and tell the one that asked the question that you don't know. If the question appertains to something that you can obtain an answer to afterwards say so. Perversely, such honestly is usually admired. It is as if your listeners are thinking, 'oh, good, (s)he's not Einstein after all, (s)he's just like the rest of us.'

If you do promise to get some information, be sure to do so.

The internal guidance system uses deviations to generate corrective commands to fly the aircraft from a position where it is to a position where it isn't. The aircraft arrives at the position where it wasn't, thus the position where it was is the position where it isn't. In the event that the position where it is now is not the same as the position where it originally wasn't, the system will acquire a variation (variations are caused by external factors and discussions of these factors is beyond the scope of this simple explanation).

CLARITY (!)

For this gem, taken from an aircraft electronics manual, I am indebted to the house journal of the Institute of Scientific and Technical Communicators.

It is a perfect example of the author assuming knowledge on the part of the reader.

Never be guilty of such a 'simple explanation' in the spoken or written word.

Paragraphs Verbal Noun Passive
Sentences Long
Words Verb
Difficult
Avoid jargon
Language Cliches
Avoid
Keep it Simple Like the Plague!!

THE CLARITY INDEX

We have established that long words and long sentences make things more difficult to understand. This applies whether we are reading or listening.

It is possible to measure this degree of difficulty by applying what is known as the "Clarity Index".

As your presentation must be written out in full at the preparation stage, you can apply the Clarity Index and measure both the degree of difficulty it contains and also the educational level needed to comfortably understand it.

HOW TO WORK IT OUT?
Work out the average sentence length:-

1. Choose a sample of 200 words.
2. Count the number of major punctuation marks . : ; ! ? —
3. Divide the number of punctuation marks into the number of words. This will give you the average sentence length in words per "sentence".
4. Record this average sentence length.

Find the percentage of long words:-

5. Underline all the long words in your sample. These are words which have three syllables or more.

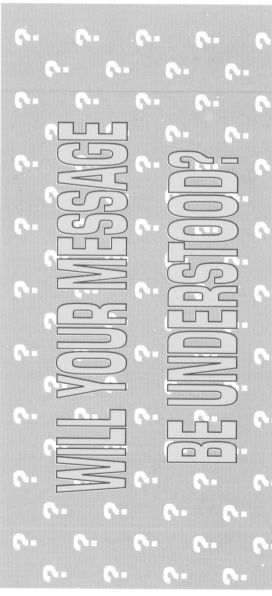

WILL YOUR MESSAGE BE UNDERSTOOD?

6. Work out the percentage of long words. In a 200 word sample halve the total number of long words counted: i.e. if there are 40 long words the count is 20%.
7. Record this percentage
8. Add the average sentence length to the percentage of long words (4 + 7).

This gives the **CLARITY INDEX.**

HOW TO USE IT
– THE INDEX IN PRACTICE:

If the index is below 20 the text is probably too abrupt and staccato.

Over 40 means that there is probably too much padding. The ideas become less clear and it may be difficult to read. Look for signs of long sentences and long words.

Most people in conversation subconsciously use an index of about 30; the average index of a whole range of newspaper editorials on any one day is about 30.

As a rough rule of thumb, if you bear the listener in mind and write as you would speak, your index will be around 30.

The accent is on understanding comfortably. Understanding without strain. If this is achieved by the presenter there is a great chance that the participants will not only understand but possibly enjoy, yes enjoy, the experience.

TO DETERMINE THE MINIMUM EDUCATION LEVEL REQUIRED TO UNDERSTAND THE WRITING TO WHICH THE CLARITY INDEX HAS BEEN APPLIED

1. Divide the Clarity Index (CI) by four and add 4. The resultant figure will represent the number of years education required *to comfortably understand* the piece of writing.

	CI	Years in Education
a.	30	11.5
b	36	13.0
c.	44	15.0
d.	50	16.25

a. CI 30 would be understood by the majority of people. All it requires is 11.5 years of education.
b. CI 36 would only be understood by those having a complete secondary education.
c. To understand this comfortably one would have to have at least completed third level education.
d. Possibly only understood comfortably by those who make a career of formal learning.

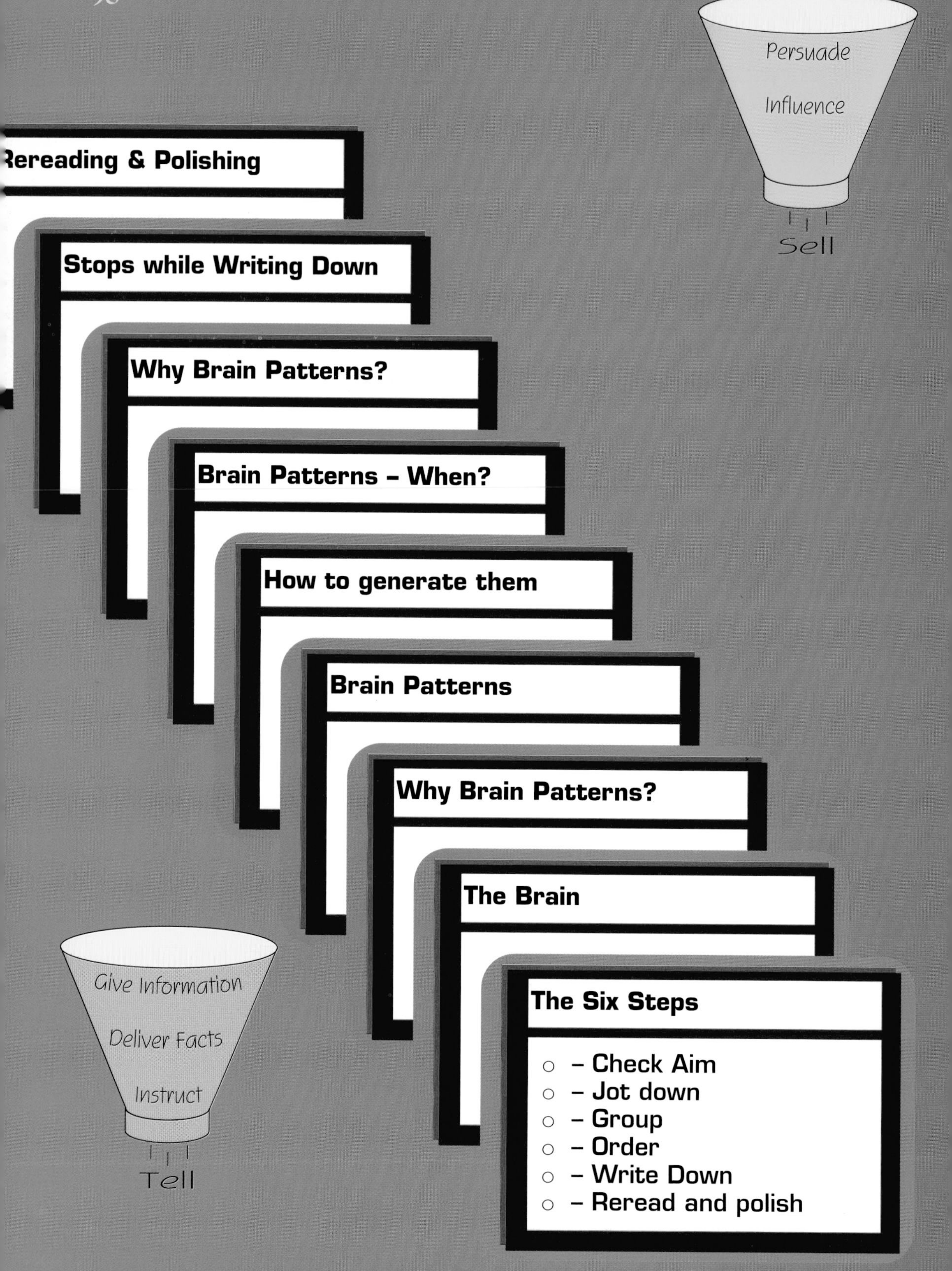

58

Persuade

Influence

Sell

Rereading & Polishing

Stops while Writing Down

Why Brain Patterns?

Brain Patterns – When?

How to generate them

Brain Patterns

Why Brain Patterns?

The Brain

Give Information

Deliver Facts

Instruct

Tell

The Six Steps

- o – Check Aim
- o – Jot down
- o – Group
- o – Order
- o – Write Down
- o – Reread and polish

Structure

The 'getting-your-act-together section of preparation. The part that probably many presenters dread. Here is where you are sitting in front of that blank piece of paper and suffering in one of two ways. Either the ideas won't come at all or they arrive so quickly that you cannot capture them before they are forgotten.

Here is where a knowledge of pattern notes can make all the difference. Your brain is not restricted to logical thinking but can freely range over the subject at will. It does not have to worry about sentences and paragraphs. Ideas and key-words are the order of the day.

Consciousness of the benefit of pattern notes and awareness that there are basically only two types of presentations helps to remove the suffering from this aspect of presentations.

This section could well be called the "getting-your-act-together" section.

It is vital to establish and crystallize your aim before you begin. It is important to express your ideas clearly in simple language.

Our aim tells us clearly what we want to say.

Using the proper language makes sure we get that message across in an understandable way.

Structuring properly ensures that the subject is covered in the most understandable way for the audience. Also that the audience will react in the way we would wish.

BASICALLY, THERE ARE BUT TWO KINDS OF PRESENTATIONS
The aim will be:

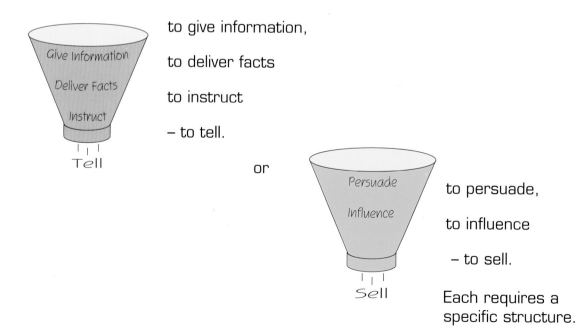

to give information,

to deliver facts

to instruct

– to tell.

or

to persuade,

to influence

– to sell.

Each requires a specific structure.

Your aim in making the presentation will decide which structure to use.

So, before structuring your presentation, check once more what your aim is.

Both types of presentation will contain basically the same information. Each will have a beginning, a middle and an end.
There is not that great a difference in content.
It is only the order of that information that will change as the diagram on the next page clearly shows. Checking the aim at this stage will also keep in mind the type of audience for whom your presentation is being prepared.

For most understandable Language check Aim

For most appropriate Structure check Aim

For best Layout check Aim

For most suitable Techniques check Aim

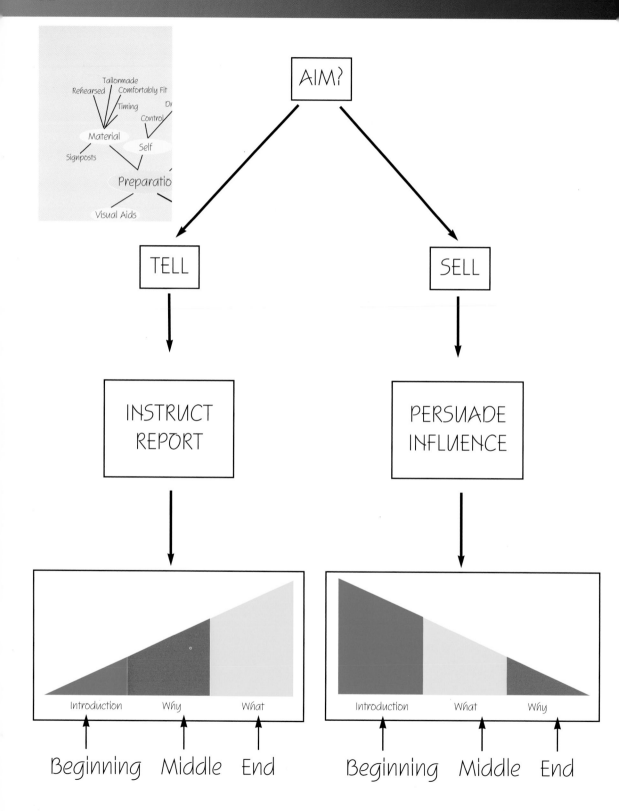

	BEGINNING	MIDDLE	END
TELL	Setting the scene Introduction and overall picture Terms of reference Background Scope	Conclusions Recommendations Action to which you require audience to agree	Details which amplify Reasoning Results of tests (All these may be brought out in a question-and-answer session)
SELL	Setting the scene Introduction and overall picture Terms of reference Background Scope	Audience is led through a logical sequence of thought before arriving at conclusion Identify the problem/situation Solve problem Show proof of solution/benefits	Conclusions Recommendations Action you require audience to agree to – having led them through the reasoning in the MIDDLE

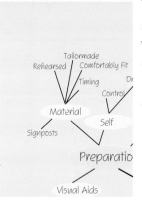

There are six simple steps which, if followed, ensure that all necessary points are covered in a logical manner.

The Six Steps

- ☑ – Check aim
- ☑ – Jot down
- ☑ – Group
- ☑ – Order
- ☑ – Write down
- ☑ – Reread and polish

HERE ARE THE STEPS:

1. **CHECK THE AIM AGAIN**

2. **JOT DOWN ALL THE IDEAS** you might like to include. Don't evaluate. The object is quantity, not quality.

    (If you 'dry up' let your eyes roam over the ideas you have already captured. Apply Kipling's honest serving men (mentioned under The Aim).

    Answers to any one of these will soon get you moving again.

3. **GROUP THE IDEAS** under headings. (If you use the pattern notes method you will have automatically grouped your ideas as you proceed. (Pages 10 and 11 are my preparation for this book.)

4. **DECIDE THE ORDER** (which will be, again, dependent on your aim).

5. **WRITE OUT YOUR PRESENTATION IN FULL** and keep the language simple.

6. **REREAD AND POLISH** your presentation.

The Brain

Automatic operations
Do not require conscious brain work

Non-Automatic operations
Require conscious brain work

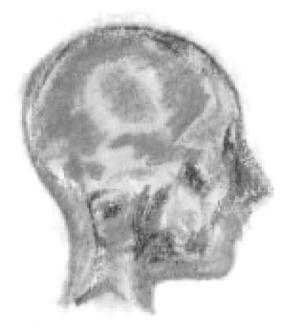

The brain carries out two kinds of operations:

1. AUTOMATIC OPERATIONS. The things you 'do without thinking' such as digesting your food etc., as well as repetitive operations, be they manual or mental.

2. NON-AUTOMATIC OPERATIONS where the brain is consciously involved in the process.

    Thinking is, of course, an example of this.

The brain can only perform one non-automatic operation at a time.

The first four points in our six steps involve thinking. The last two might be classed as automatic as they only involve writing.

Trouble with structuring comes because we mix up thinking and writing. We try to do two things at the same time.

Distinguish between automatic and non-automatic mental work and give your brain a chance

The six-point plan separates both these actions and allows your brain to devote its full attention to the action in hand.

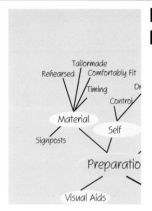

BRAIN PATTERNS

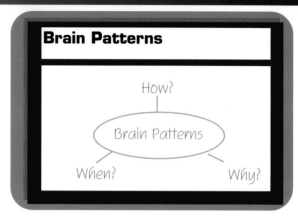

WHY BRAIN PATTERNS ARE GOOD

1. You can work in a style closer to the 3-D way in your brain works.
2. Brain patterns allow your mind to wander at random.
3. You do not lose ideas that occur at the 'wrong' time or 'wrong' place.
4. You can develop or extend a train of thought at any time.
5. They allow you to clear mental blocks.
6. They allow you to collect and group all your ideas at once.

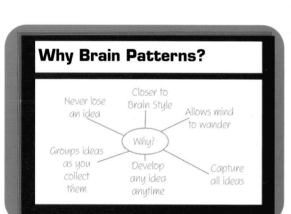

HOW TO GENERATE THEM

1. Start in the middle of a page.
2. Note all ideas as they occur.
3. Some ideas occur randomly and need to be noted immediately.
4. At other times you can follow and develop a train of thought and can let your ideas grow out from the centre of the page like a tree's branches and twigs.
5. Try not to stop writing. Keep the ideas flowing by returning to an earlier thought and developing that if you do dry up for ideas.

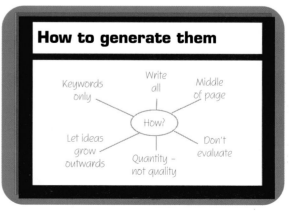

Brain Patterns remove the strictures attached to logical thinking. This allows your brain to free range over the whole subject picking up all ideas as they occur.

There is no such thing as 'I'm not ready for that idea yet'. You capture all your ideas first, then place them in order at a later stage.

Why Brain Patterns?

Brain Patterns allow you to capture ideas.
Once you have the ideas the words will follow.
Ideas are often lost in "usual writing" while the words are been written down.

Brain Patterns – When?

WHEN TO USE BRAIN PATTERNS

1. Planning - anything and everything that needs to be planned.
2. Solving problems - analysing worries.
3. Preparing presentations, reports and memos, speeches, notes etc.
4. Revising.
5. To mark and check off progress and achievement.
6. Preparing for meetings.

When you are working with brain patterns you spend most of your thinking time and all of your writing time on ideas.
When you try to prepare in the normal way your writing cannot keep up with the speed at which your brain can generate ideas. Therefore many excellent ideas and arguments are lost – possibly forever.

REMEMBER WHEN YOU BEGIN WRITING DOWN:

Writing Down

This is where presenters are inclined to 'rush it'

Time taken here is time well spent

Stops while Writing Down

You have not spent enough time at #2. Go back to these notes again

1. If you find yourself continually stopping because you are thinking of other ideas for the presentation, then you have not devoted sufficient time to point two (jotting down).

2. If you are aware of lengthy sentences (especially ones that are lengthened by the conjunction 'and'), this also means that you did not spend long enough at the jotting-down stage.

Writing Down

Lengthy sentences are difficult for you to deliver – and for your listeners to understand

---

Rereading and Polishing

Reread in a questioning frame of mind. In this way you will be looking to improve all the time.

The final part is the rereading and polishing of the script. This is at least as vital as anything else in the preparation.

TIMING

One of the problems that rears its ugly head over and over again is the business of timing.

Presenters say that no matter how often they rehearse and time their material, they find themselves running out of time when delivering the actual presentation.

This problem can usually be traced back directly to point 6 of the structuring.
Reread and polish.

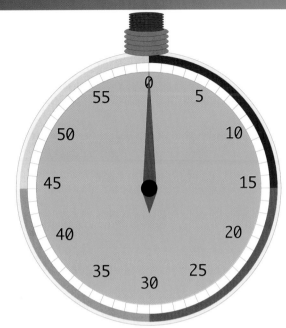

Many are inclined to time themselves while rereading silently. They forget that, although most of us can read comfortably at 200 words per minute, it is difficult to attain an average of even 45 words a minute when speaking to a group. You must allow for emphasis, reaction and audience participation.

Also, when reading silently, sentences that would be difficult to deliver when speaking out loud pose no problems.

Reread out loud

You can read comfortably at 200 words per minute. Delivering your presentation you will be lucky to maintain 40 words per minute

The message is clear. When rehearsing it is vital that you rehearse out loud and allow for audience reaction, participation and questions.

Stick to the 80%-20% Rule and this problem will disappear.

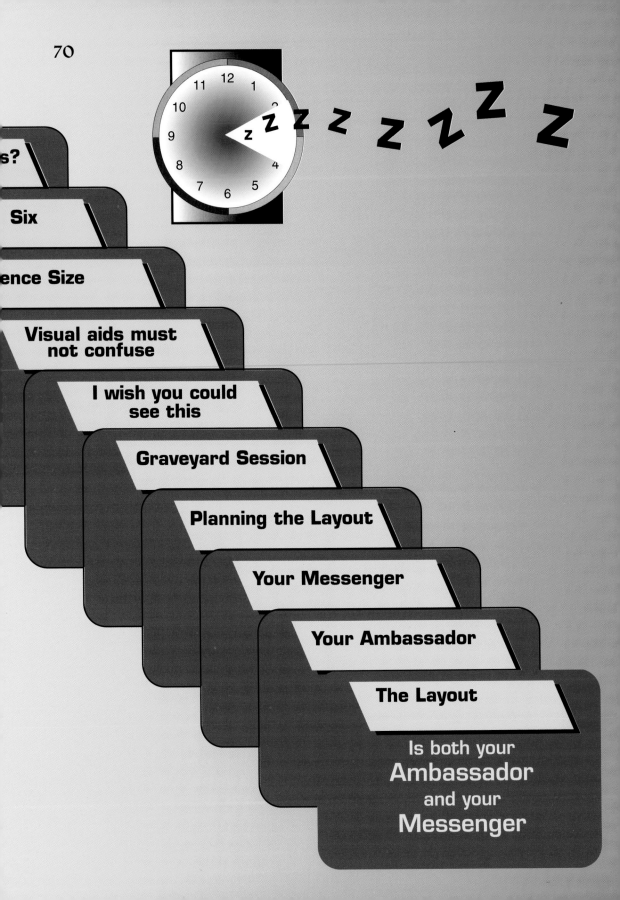

...s?

Six

...ence Size

Visual aids must not confuse

I wish you could see this

Graveyard Session

Planning the Layout

Your Messenger

Your Ambassador

The Layout

Is both your
Ambassador
and your
Messenger

Layout

Here is where you add appeal to your presentation. You will be judged, possibly subconsciously, on the standard of your visual aids and other course material. That is why your material must fill the dual roles of both messenger and ambassador. Not only must it get your message across but it also creates the impression – good or bad – of you and the organization you represent.

Knowing of the Rule of Six gives you two advantages. It prevents you cluttering up your slides or transparencies. It also encourages you to present your visual aids in a manner that your audience will find most receptive.

Remember always that your objective always is to express yourself clearly and therefore there should be neither ambiguity nor confusion in your visual aids or course material.

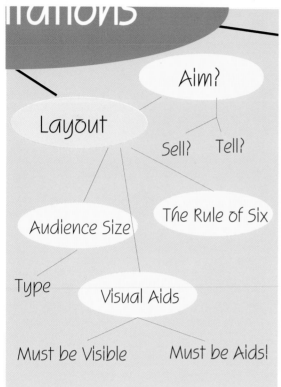

llations

Aim?

Layout

Sell? Tell?

The Rule of Six

Audience Size

Type

Visual Aids

Must be Visible   Must be Aids!

There is a saying in the training business that you are only as good as your last presentation.

Past endorsements pale beside the assessment of your latest presentation by its participants.

Therefore your next course or presentation must always be the best one you have ever delivered.

Bear this in mind all the while you are preparing.

Your presentation also fulfils two additional roles.

It is both your ambassador and your messenger.

Layout

Your Presentation is
Your Ambassador
and
Your Messenger

Layout

Your Ambassador

it creates the impression
– **Of You** and
– **Your Organization**

IT IS YOUR AMBASSADOR because it creates the impression of you and your organization.

If your presentation is enjoyed and informative the kudos will reflect on both you and your organization. The corollary is also true.

IT IS YOUR MESSENGER also because it is the vehicle you are using to get your message across.

Unless both these roles are fulfilled your presentation cannot be considered a 100% success.

Layout

Your Messenger
It is the vehicle you use to get your message across

Time spent planning your layout will be repaid a hundred fold.

Layout

Time spent planning the layout will be repaid one hundred fold

It is one of the keys to successful presentations

PLANNING THE LAYOUT

Again, begin by referring back to the aim and keep it in mind right through the planning.

As the layout will depend on it, establish whether it could be classed as informative or persuasive. Follow the rules of Tell or Sell here.

Layout

Planning the layout:
- ☑ – Check aim
- ☑ – Is it Tell or Sell?
- ☑ – Group size?
- ☑ – Auditorium
- ☑ – Time of day?

Obtain some information on the auditorium. Basically, the less comfortable the seating, the more interesting the presentation must be.

Time of day is also important as the attention span varies with the time of day.

At the beginning of a day-long presentation, the attention level is usually high. Enthusiasm for the subject usually sees to this. This enthusiasm can be maintained. It flags slightly approaching the mid-morning break but is high again

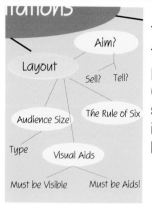

The danger time from the presenter's point of view is the session beginning immediately after lunch.

This period is usually referred to by presenters and trainers as 'the graveyard session'. The participants have completed the morning sessions and probably eaten a full lunch. This combination usually tends to make them unattentive and 'soporific'. An exciting, interesting session is the best counteraction to this.

MAKE SURE THAT ALL THE VISUAL AIDS YOU USE ARE BOTH VISUAL AND ARE AIDS

We have all witnessed a presenter hold up an article while saying something like "I wish you could all see this because it really emphasizes what I have been saying…"

Again, presenters are still inclined to project A4-filled pages of typescript in the usual 10-point type and expect their audience to be able to read them.

Visual aids should be exactly that.

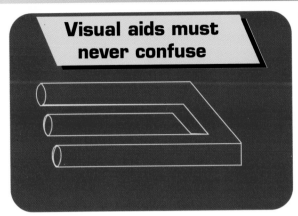

Visual aids must never confuse

Visual aids should be exactly that.

If it is essential that you refer to specific documents to make a certain point, include these in the manual or course notes. Don't confuse your audience by trying to show them on screen.

Here are some more questions you should answer before determining your layout:

Layout

The larger the audience

The plainer the slide

SIZE OF AUDIENCE?
– Will it be a small intimate presentation to a single figure audience or must you cater for hundreds? ✓

– Which medium will it be most appropriate?:

  – Overhead projector? ✓

  – 35mm slides? ✓

  – On-screen presentation? ✓

A complex design may look quite natural to a group of five looking at your monitor, but the same design may seem very cluttered to someone sitting in the back row of an auditorium. Similarly, overheads, unless computer driven, may not be suitable for larger audiences but would probably be ideal for, say, a board meeting, or a small group.

These are points that many presenters never consider. They make a presentation and it is a tremendous success. The performance is repeated to similar sizes and types of audiences and is equally successful. Then the size of audience is dramatically increased or decreased (or the type of audience changes) and the presentation turns out to be a flop – and the presenter cannot figure out why.

THE RULE OF SIX

Tests carried out in educational departments of universities have proved that the brain can more easily absorb information if it is presented in not more than six items at a time.

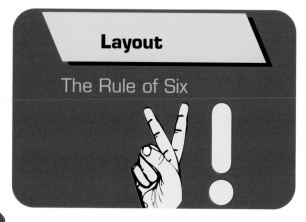

We can use this to advantage. Ensure there are never more than six sub-headings or points under any heading.

If you find you have more than six look

Layout

The Rule of Six.

☑ – Maximum of six sub headings.

☑ – Maximum of six points under any sub-heading.

at your heading again. Maybe the heading is not definitive enough. Maybe there should be two or more headings?

Layout

More than six points?

☑ – Is the heading specific enough?

☑ – Should there be two or more headings?

Sir Winston Churchill was asked once why he thought his speeches were so successful.

"It's simple", he replied, "I speak simply and more than half the time I am speaking – I say nothing!"

Keep it simple

I have nothing to offer but...
Sanguinity,
Perspiration
and
Mournful Sorrow!

What he meant was that the pauses in his speeches actually occupied more time than the actual words – and this did not just happen – he planned his speeches this way.

Remember, not only when speaking but when preparing your slides.

How about...
Blood,
Sweat
and Tears?

Open spaces are as important as the content. Let 'less is more' be your watchword when you come to planning the individual slides.

Use several slides. Better still, use slide-builds to animate your bulleted points. Then each one is presented separately and has its own impact

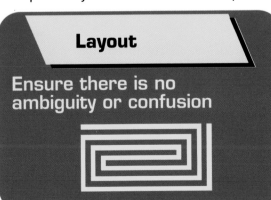

Layout

Ensure there is no ambiguity or confusion

KEEP IT SIMPLE

Lastly, keep your layout simple. Avoid ambiguity or confusion.

Try to let your eyes follow the line in the slide on the left and see what happens!

Butterfly
or
caterpillar?

!

– It's entirely up to you!

ng their attention

Converting artwork

Colour tables

Colour combinations

Master slides

Colour adds impact

Coping with boredom

Avoid boring your audience

Use Your Assets

Yourself:

Your appearance
Your enthusiasm
Your confidence
Your presence

Techniques

All the time and effort you have put into getting your presentation together will come to nought unless you can grab and hold the attention of your audience.

You must be always alert to spot boredom appearing in your group (yawning, twiddling pens and pencils, gazing into middle-distance, reading while you are speaking, talking to others while you are speaking, etc.).
The more interesting you and your visual aids are, the less likely your group is to drift away mentally.

Use colour. Colour adds impact to your subject. The colour combinations and tables on pages 86–89 will give you all the information you need when designing transparencies and slides.

Don't be afraid to remind your group that learning is a two-way process that requires their active co-operation for success.

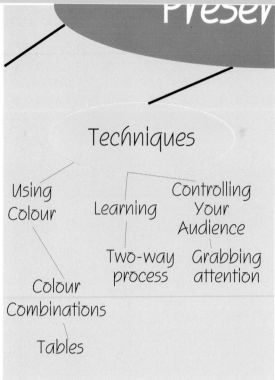

Preser

Techniques

Using Colour

Learning

Controlling Your Audience

Two-way process

Grabbing attention

Colour Combinations

Tables

To a great extent, the tools you use to get your message across will depend on your audience and the facilities available in the auditorium, boardroom or lecture theatre.

Nowadays, thanks to improvements in technology, you can connect up your computer directly to the overhead projector or to a large screen.

With a little practice your computer can take the place of almost all the other methods from black and white boards through 35mm projectors.

You have other assets that can be used to great advantage:

•YOURSELF

Your own confidence as you begin can permeate through the audience – and give them confidence in you. Never underestimate this.

Be excited about your subject. Excitement is catching.

Use Your Assets

Yourself:

> **Your appearance**
> **Your enthusiasm**
> **Your confidence**
> **Your presence**

Use Your Assets

Your ability to:

> o – **sense the mood**
> o – **vary the pace**
> o – **change the subject**
> o – **ask questions**

Your ability to sense the mood of the group – particularly with regard to their interest level – will ensure you know when to vary the pace, change the subject or ask that question that will re-awake interest in your listeners.

- From the beginning, use people's names, particularly with smaller groups – and ask questions. Nothing cements a group and puts it in the right frame of mind faster than feeling they are recognized.

- **SEATING**
- Your choices in this respect are limited with larger audiences.

  With smaller groups, arrange the seating in a U-shape. Now no-one is at the front or back of the room. Also everyone can see the rest of the group.

Group Participation

If the group is not inclined to participate, take off your jacket and roll up your sleeves as you continue. You will find that your audience will mentally take off their jackets and participate as you wish.

Similarly, if the group is tending to become obstreperous, as you continue, roll down your sleeves and re-don your jacket. The group will subconsciously recognize that the degree of formality has increased and react accordingly.

Colour

Use of colour in the make-up of your visual aids can often bring a certain amount of excitement to what otherwise might be termed the dullest subject.

Make sure the colours you use 'balance' with each other. In this book I have varied the background and script colours in the slides in various sections to show you some good possible combinations. Colour is dealt with in greater depth in this section.

Your objective with colour should be to catch the eye - not bedazzle your audience.

Using pastel shades in the manuals also allows you to easily observe who might be moving ahead of the posse - the sheets he/she is reading will be a different shade.

AVOIDING BORING YOUR AUDIENCE

Yes, it can happen – and you must make sure you know if it is happening.

Lack of preparation on your part (We're back to Aim again) can cause boredom. It can also be caused by having to explain something to a few in the audience that is already understood by the majority.

Whereas you can actually see when you are boring the smaller audience and can take immediate action, it is not as easy with larger groups.

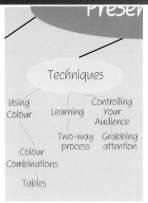

Techniques

Using Colour

Learning

Controlling Your Audience

Two-way process

Grabbing attention

Colour Combinations

Tables

COPING WITH BOREDOM

For the larger audiences especially, I use the 'yellow card'. In Association Football the referee shows a yellow card to warn a player that he has committed an offence and will be 'sent off' if he commits the same offence again.

In the material presented to the candidates when they arrived would be a yellow card of approximately postcard-size. This card would be blank, except for eight small squares

I explain to the group:

"You will notice that on one side of your card are three groups of blank squares; a single square, a double square and a group of five squares. Hold the card so that the single square is on the left hand side.

Now write the letter 'B' in the fourth square from the left and the letter 'E' in the seventh square. Next put the letter 'M' in the third square and the letter 'D' in the eighth square". (By this stage I can see smiles appearing on some faces.) "In the second square place an 'A', an 'O' in the fifth square, an 'I' in the first square and, lastly, an 'R' in the sixth square."

Your audience can now see that what is spelled out is:

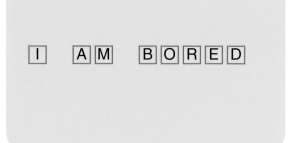

I explain that it is not always easy to see if I happen to be boring more than one or two people.

As I don't have any right to bore them, this card should be used in more or less the same way as the referee uses the yellow card.

If they are bored they should raise the yellow card.

Try it – it works!

COLOUR ADDS IMPACT TO YOUR PRESENTATION

- Use colour sparingly.
  This enhances your message.

- Warm colours are best used as accents.

- Cool colours can be used more freely.

- If you plan to use colour in text, check the legibility of the colours. For example, yellow on a white background is difficult to read.

THIS IS A MOST
IMPORTANT NOTICE

**THIS IS A MOST
IMPORTANT NOTICE**

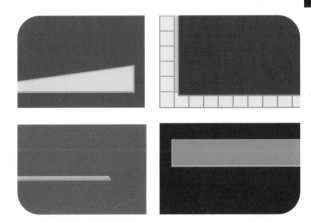

- For slide backgrounds, choose dark colours and solid patterns.

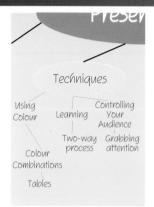

MASTER SLIDES

The presentation program that I have a particular preference for is Aldus Persuasion.

It is simple to learn and allows you to import information from a variety of sources. Likewise, it also allows you export to other programs. They have thought of everything:

- Master slides to control the look of your slides. These contain 'place holders'. These specify where your text will go; its size and how it will be justified. Any or all may be over-ridden by you.

- You can create new slides from scratch or base your slides on an outline. Once you have the text inserted, the default master you assign will format that text and create the slide.

- Other forms that regularly cause trouble are graphics and organization charts. Aldus has taken the headaches out of these aspects also.

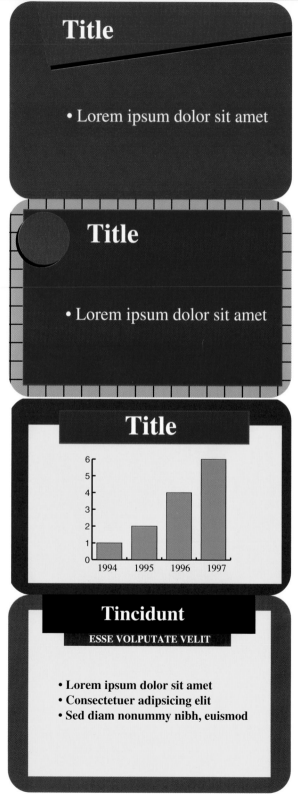

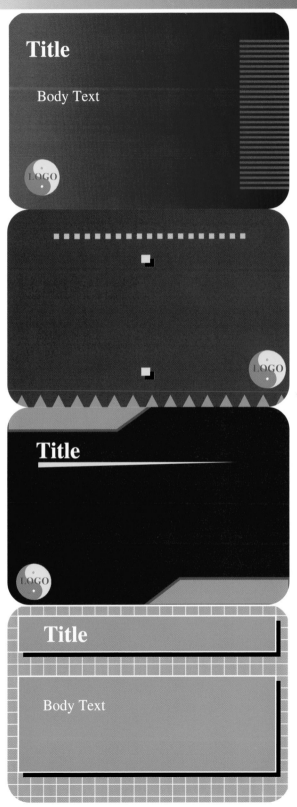

- The program allows you to animate by giving you the facility of setting out your information on different layers.

- There are also background masters. They can contain graphics, static text and can be filled with patterns or colours.

- I have another personal reason for liking this program. Like ten per cent of the male population I am red-green colour-blind.

The back-up material includes a very handy desktop reference which gives details of colour schemes and details which colours blend best with others. The examples on pages 78–81 are based on these.

I can make my presentation with a computer connected to a large screen, or overhead projector. Such presentations can be simply converted into 35mm slides.

There are also a series of Autotemplates. The backgrounds illustrated on these two pages are based on some of them. If time is short, no matter what the subject of your presentation is, you can find a ready-made format to suit.

A BACKGROUND: C:100 Y: 90 M :10 K: 0

	1	2	3	4
	5	6	7	8
	9	10	11	12
	13	14	15	16

	%C	%M	%Y	%K	SHADE
1	0	0	0	100	100%
2					
3	100	0	55	0	100%
4	100	80	40	0	30%
5	5	20	95	0	100%
6	100	90	10	0	90%
7	80	5	0	0	100%
8	80	5	0	0	60%
9	0	100	90	0	90%
10	25	100	25	0	100%
11	100	0	0	0	100%
12	75	5	100	0	60%
13	45	90	0	0	70%
14	45	90	0	0	80%
15	0	0	0	100	40%
16	75	5	100	0	100%

	%C	%M	%Y	%K	SHADE
1	0	0	0	100	100%
2					
3	0	100	0	0	100%
4	75	90	0	0	30%
5	45	90	0	0	90%
6	45	90	0	0	30%
7	100	0	55	0	90%
8	100	0	55	0	60%
9	100	95	0	0	70%
10	100	95	0	0	40%
11	0	25	100	0	70%
12	75	25	100	0	50%
13	80	5	0	0	60%
14	80	5	0	0	50%
15	0	80	100	10	90%
16	0	80	100	10	40%

B BACKGROUND: C: 75 Y: 90 M : 0 K: 0

	%C	%M	%Y	%K	SHADE
1	0	0	0	100	100%
2					
3	0	100	0	0	100%
4	0	0	100	0	40%
5	25	100	25	0	60%
6	25	100	25	0	40%
7	75	5	100	0	80%
8	75	5	100	0	30%
9	75	90	0	0	60%
10	75	90	0	0	30%
11	100	0	55	0	80%
12	100	0	55	0	30%
13	100	95	0	0	70%
14	100	95	0	0	30%
15	0	0	0	100	60%
16	0	0	0	100	30%

C BACKGROUND: C: 0 Y: 0 M: 0 K: 80

	1	2	3	4
	5	6	7	8
	9	10	11	12
	13	14	15	16

	%C	%M	%Y	%K	SHADE
1	0	0	0	100	20%
2					
3	0	100	0	0	100%
4	0	0	0	100	60%
5	0	25	100	0	80%
6	0	25	100	0	60%
7	45	90	0	0	70%
8	45	90	0	0	40%
9	0	45	100	0	80%
10	0	45	100	0	60%
11	100	95	0	0	80%
12	100	95	0	0	50%
13	15	100	100	0	60%
14	15	100	100	0	40%
15	75	5	100	00	80%
16	75	5	100	00	60%

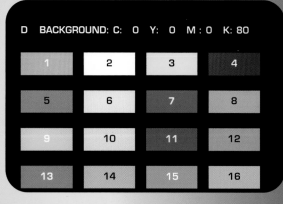

D BACKGROUND: C: 0 Y: 0 M : 0 K: 80

	%C	%M	%Y	%K	SHADE
1	0	0	0	100	100%
2					
3	0	100	0	0	100%
4	25	100	25	0	30%
5	25	100	25	0	60%
6	25	100	25	0	30%
7	75	5	100	0	80%
8	75	5	100	0	40%
9	0	0	100	0	80%
10	0	0	100	0	40%
11	100	95	0	0	60%
12	100	95	0	0	30%
13	100	0	55	0	80%
14	100	0	55	0	60%
15	0	0	0	100	60%
16	0	0	0	100	30%

E BACKGROUND: C: 25 Y:100 M :25 K: 0

1	2	3	4
5	6	7	8
9	10	11	12
13	14	15	16

F BACKGROUND: C: 75 Y: 5 M :100 K: 0

1	2	3	4
5	6	7	8
9	10	11	12
13	14	15	16

	%C	%M	%Y	%K	SHADE
1	0	0	0	100	100%
2					
3	0	100	0	0	100%
4	75	5	100	0	30%
5	75	5	100	0	70%
6	75	5	100	0	40%
7	45	90	0	0	60%
8	45	90	0	0	30%
9	0	100	90	0	90%
10	25	100	25	0	100%
11	0	100	0	0	70%
12	0	100	0	0	30%
13	100	95	0	0	70%
14	100	95	0	0	30%
15	0	25	100	0	70%
16	0	25	100	0	40%

	%C	%M	%Y	%K	SHADE
1	0	0	0	100	100%
2					
3	0	100	0	0	100%
4	100	95	0	0	30%
5	100	0	55	0	80%
6	100	0	55	0	50%
7	45	90	0	0	50%
8	45	90	0	0	30%
9	75	5	100	0	80%
10	75	5	100	0	40%
11	0	100	0	0	80%
12	0	100	0	0	40%
13	80	5	0	0	70%
14	80	5	0	0	40%
15	0	80	100	10	70%
16	0	80	100	10	40%

G BACKGROUND: C:100 Y: 95 M : 0 K: 0

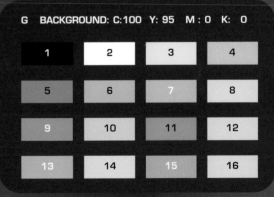

1	2	3	4
5	6	7	8
9	10	11	12
13	14	15	16

H BACKGROUND: C: 50 M:85 Y :100 K: 0

1	2	3	4
5	6	7	8
9	10	11	12
13	14	15	16

	%C	%M	%Y	%K	SHADE
1	0	0	0	100	100%
2					
3	0	100	0	0	100%
4	50	85	100	0	50%
5	0	25	100	0	80%
6	0	25	100	0	50%
7	75	90	0	0	60%
8	75	90	0	0	30%
9	15	100	100	0	70%
10	15	100	100	0	40%
11	100	95	0	0	80%
12	100	95	0	0	30%
13	0	100	0	0	80%
14	0	100	0	0	40%
15	75	0	100	0	80%
16	75	0	100	0	60%

I BACKGROUND: C: 80 M: 5 Y :10 K: 0

	%C	%M	%Y	%K	SHADE
1	0	0	0	100	100%
2					
3	0	100	0	0	100%
4	100	95	0	0	100%
5	0	80	100	10	70%
6	0	80	100	10	40%
7	45	90	0	0	70%
8	45	90	0	0	40%
9	15	100	100	0	70%
10	15	100	100	0	40%
11	80	5	0	0	80%
12	80	5	100	0	40%
13	0	0	100	0	80%
14	0	0	100	0	40%
15	75	5	100	0	90%
16	75	5	100	0	40%

	%C	%M	%Y	%K	SHADE
1	0	0	0	100	100%
2					
3	0	100	0	0	100%
4	0	0	100	0	50%
5	0	25	100	0	70%
6	0	25	100	0	30%
7	0	0	100	0	80%
8	0	0	100	0	30%
9	0	80	100	10	60%
10	0	80	100	10	30%
11	45	90	0	0	70%
12	45	90	0	0	20%
13	15	100	100	0	70%
14	15	100	100	0	30%
15	100	95	0	0	60%
16	100	95	0	10	20%

J BACKGROUND: C:100 M: 0 Y :55 K: 0

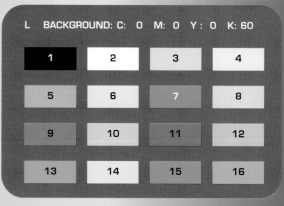

	%C	%M	%Y	%K	SHADE
1	0	0	0	100	100%
2					
3	0	100	0	0	100%
4	0	100	0	0	50%
5	0	25	100	0	70%
6	0	25	100	0	30%
7	100	95	0	0	70%
8	100	95	0	0	50%
9	100	50	0	0	80%
10	100	50	0	0	60%
11	0	100	0	0	80%
12	0	100	0	0	20%
13	80	5	0	0	80%
14	80	5	0	0	50%
15	75	0	100	0	80%
16	75	0	100	0	40%

K BACKGROUND: C: 0 M:100 Y : 0 K: 0

	%C	%M	%Y	%K	SHADE
1	0	0	0	100	100%
2					
3	0	100	0	0	100%
4	0	0	100	0	50%
5	0	80	100	10	60%
6	0	80	100	10	30%
7	45	90	0	0	70%
8	45	90	0	0	30%
9	50	85	100	0	70%
10	50	85	100	0	30%
11	100	95	0	0	60%
12	100	95	0	0	30%
13	0	100	0	0	70%
14	0	100	0	0	30%
15	75	0	100	00	80%
16	75	0	100	00	60%

L BACKGROUND: C: 0 M: 0 Y: 0 K: 60

	%C	%M	%Y	%K	SHADE
1	0	0	0	100	100%
2					
3	0	100	0	0	100%
4	0	25	100	0	60%
5	0	80	100	10	60%
6	15	100	100	0	60%
7	80	5	0	0	60%
8	75	5	100	0	70%
9	25	100	25	0	70%
10	45	90	0	0	60%
11	100	0	55	0	70%
12	75	5	100	0	70%
13	75	90	0	0	60%
14	100	95	0	0	60%
15	0	0	0	100	60%
16	0	0	0	100	20%

BACKGROUND: White

1	2	3	4
5	6	7	8
9	10	11	12
13	14	15	16

	%C	%M	%Y	%K	SHADE
1	0	0	0	100	100%
2					
3	0	100	0	0	100%
4	100	95	0	0	100%
5	0	80	100	10	60%
6	0	80	100	10	40%
7	45	90	0	0	60%
8	45	90	0	0	40%
9	100	55	100	0	60%
10	100	55	100	0	40%
11	100	95	0	0	60%
12	100	95	0	0	40%
13	0	100	0	0	80%
14	0	100	0	0	40%
15	100	0	55	0	80%
16	100	0	55	0	60%

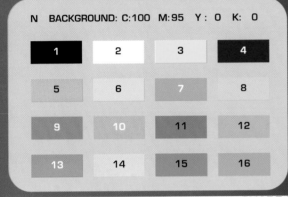

N BACKGROUND: C:100 M:95 Y:0 K:0

	%C	%M	%Y	%K	SHADE
1	0	0	0	100	100%
2					
3	0	100	0	0	100%
4	100	55	100	0	20%
5	100	95	0	0	60%
6	100	95	0	0	50%
7	15	100	100	0	60%
8	15	100	100	0	30%
9	45	90	0	0	60%
10	45	90	0	0	40%
11	0	80	100	0	60%
12	0	80	100	0	40%
13	0	0	100	0	60%
14	0	0	100	0	40%
15	100	0	55	0	80%
16	100	0	55	0	60%

O BACKGROUND: C:100 M:55 Y:100 K:0

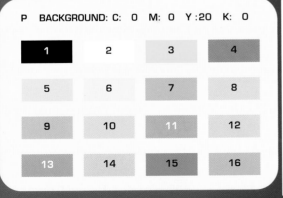

P BACKGROUND: C:0 M:0 Y:20 K:0

	%C	%M	%Y	%K	SHADE
1	0	0	0	100	100%
2					
3	0	100	0	0	100%
4	50	85	100	0	70%
5	0	25	100	0	60%
6	0	25	100	0	40%
7	0	100	0	0	60%
8	0	100	0	0	40%
9	0	80	100	10	60%
10	0	80	100	10	40%
11	45	90	0	0	50%
12	45	90	0	0	30%
13	25	100	25	0	60%
14	25	100	25	0	40%
15	100	0	25	0	80%
16	100	0	25	0	50%

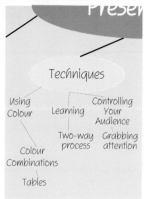

CONVERTING ARTWORK

I also use computer generated drawings, scanned images and pixel artwork. All clip-art is converted into line drawings and changed and coloured with the use of Adobe Illustrator. Adobe Illustrator also allows me to produce further special effects.

The disadvantage of pixel artwork is that the majority of it is considered too 'rough' for the end product required by most professional users today.

For example, here is a butterfly that has been taken directly from MacPaint (figure 1).

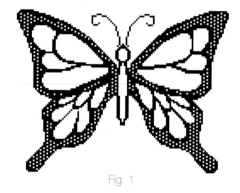

Fig. 1

Fig. 2

Here is the same butterfly after passing through Adobe Streamline (figure 2).

This conversion allows me to colour the artwork in Adobe Illustrator (figure 3.) and also make any alterations I might wish.

Fig. 3

GRABBING THEIR ATTENTION

The first thing we must do is grab the attention of our audience and make sure that they know that this presentation is a two-way process. By this I mean that your audience must actively listen.

Gaining knowledge is not just leaning back and allowing the sights and sounds created by the presenter waft over you. There's more to it than hoping that some will 'settle' in your brain, in the same way as a wave washes over a rock on the shoreline – some water settles on the rock but most of it just washes away again.

Your audience must be under no illusions.

Learning is not like the 'placing on of hands'. It requires more from them.

Geoffrey Rawlinson, the master of brainstorming, used a Tyrannosaurus Rex – the last of the great dinosaurs to make this point.

As the candidates entered the lecture theatre they would see the skeleton of the Tyrannosaurus Rex projected onto a screen towering over them. The dinosaur would dominate the lecture theatre right up to the moment the lecture began.

Geoffrey's opening remarks would be:

"Tyrannosaurus Rex, the biggest of the dinosaurs, must have thought life was perfect but he couldn't adapt to change and so he became extinct. Today, we're going to look for a way of adapting to rapid change and actually benefitting from change by anticipating it..."

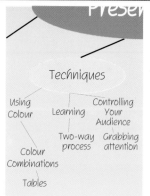

Less than fifty words but they never failed to get the desired effect.

<50

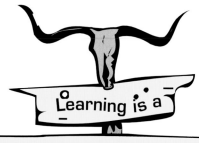

Learning is a

Two-Way Process
It requires 4 things from you

Motivation – **You must want to improve**
Confidence – **You must believe you can improve**
Effort – **You must be prepared to work for it**
Persistance – **You must be prepared to put the ideas into regular use**

In two sentences the presenter has linked up the projected image of the dinosaur and the subject of his presentation, brainstorming.

He has done more. He has started his audience thinking. They are receptive; they are ready to assist Geoffrey to assist them – I'll bet that you also began thinking as you read his words.

The first thing I want to do at every presentation is to persuade my audience that this is a two-way process and I can do nothing without their active mental participation.

I have the responsibility of presenting my material in a manner that makes it interesting and enjoyable – yes, enjoyable.

It is the audience's responsibility to listen actively and questioningly. They must also let me know if there is any premise that they do not understand. If they do not understand, they will not remember.

To get this message across I use the caterpillar and the butterfly.

I point out that to become a butterfly, the caterpillar has literally nothing to do but to wrap him or herself into a cocoon and wait.

Many of those who attend presentations seem to have the same impression. They are the caterpillars, the presentation is the cocoon and they will leave when the presentation is completed, having attained their objective without any effort on their part.

Nothing could be further from the truth.

Remember also that many of those who attend have been 'sent' there by either training managers or supervisors, without having the benefits of such a course properly explained to them.

I point out that learning is a two-way process involving the candidate and the presenter. It requires four things from the candidate: I stress the need for practice from the beginning. Those who use their new skills improve on them. Those who don't will lose most of what they gain from the presentation. .

LEARNING IS A TWO-WAY PROCESS

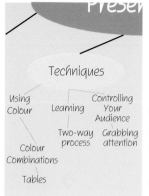

Techniques

Using Colour

Learning

Controlling Your Audience

Colour Combinations

Two-way process

Grabbing attention

Tables

Don't be afraid in an improvement or learning type presentation, to let your audience know that the buck stops with them.

You are there because you have the ability to take them successfully through this course. But you can only do this with their full cooperation. You have a track record. Others have comfortably achieved their goals on similar courses. You know how to involve the group in various discussions.

But you can only achieve your own goal with their active participation. Having informed the group at the first session that learning is a two-way process and told them the story of the caterpillar and the butterfly, I leave the slide at the bottom of this page projected when we come to the end of our first session. It is there when they leave the room for their break and it is there when they come back and while I begin the introduction to the next session.

The message always gets across.

Butterfly or caterpillar?

– It's entirely up to you!

UNDERSTANDING

For your audience to remember, it must understand what you are saying. Understanding the subject is vital for memory. Without understanding, you are relying on memorizing. This is a difficult exercise which the brain dislikes. Also, as presentations are usually structured so that ensuing topics rely on the previous one being understood, the problem is compounded for the participant as time progresses.

Encourage your group to ask questions. Remind them that there is no such thing as a 'stupid question'. From experience you will be aware of areas where difficulties arise. If questions aren't forthcoming, ask rhetorical questions.

NERVOUS?

Some presenters suffer unnecessarily from nerves because of the calibre of the audience they are to address.

One example of this might be a young graphic designer presenting a corporate identity solution to a board of directors. He or she thinks of the audience in terms of being old enough to be their father, the years of experience they have and possibly their earning – ten times as much as his or hers.

Instead of thinking like this, ask yourself: Who knows more about the subject of the presentation?

The answer to this must be the presenter. Any other answer would mean that the presentation should be given by someone else.

Index